W9-ANH-151

Twayne's United States Authors Series

Sylvia E. Bowman, *Editor*

INDIANA UNIVERSITY

Edward Albee

EDWARD ALBEE

By RICHARD E. AMACHER

Auburn University

141

Twayne Publishers, Inc. :: New York

Library of Congress Catalog Card Number: 68-24299

MANUFACTURED IN THE UNITED STATES OF AMERICA

To the memory of my father

ALBERT AMACHER

a voice of common sense
during
the Age of the Absurd

Acknowledgments

To Mr. Edward Albee, who kindly gave generous permission to quote from his plays.

To the following publishers and persons for permission to use specific printed materials: Coward-McCann, Inc., for *The American Dream, The Zoo Story, The Sandbox* and *The Death of Bessie Smith,* by Edward Albee; Atheneum Publishers for *Who's Afraid of Virginia Woolf?, Malcolm, Tiny Alice,* and *A Delicate Balance;* Houghton Mifflin Company for *The Ballad of the Sad Cafe;* The New York Times Company, as well as Mr. Albee, for "Who Is James Purdy?", an article which appeared on January 9, 1966, in the *New York Times;* Mr. Antony di Gesu and the *Saturday Review of Literature* for a portrait of Mr. Albee; the Dramatists Play Service, Inc., for *Fam and Yam.*

For purposes of clarity, all prefatory material of a descriptive nature and all stage directions from Mr. Albee's plays have been italicized, whether or not they were italicized in the originals.

Preface

IN *An Essay of Dramatic Poesy,* Dryden quotes the Latin writer Velleius to the effect that criticism of contemporary authors is difficult—" 'tis hard to judge uprightly of the living" (*Res Gestae,* II, 36). With an author as controversial as Edward Albee, the truth of this ancient saying gains greater force than ever. Albee has been subject during the past decade to considerable praise and blame—some of it deserved, and some largely unmerited. He has seemingly thriven on the critics' misunderstanding and stupidity—and, in some instances, on the downright abuse they have fired at him. And, on occasion, he has drawn spectacular attention to himself by firing back a salvo or two at his detractors.

The fact that some modern American dramatic criticism is practically valueless surely depends on the conditions under which it is written. The drama critic for a newspaper or magazine may see the play, then rush to his typewriter, and hurriedly bat out so many words to meet his deadline. In this respect the academic critic has an advantage: after seeing the play in the theater, he can take time for unhurried study of its printed text. This advantage may be the only one such a critic has, for it is without doubt true that journalist critics often have more experience and, in some cases, are far more interesting writers than the stuffy drones sometimes found buzzing away invisibly in academic hives.

Whatever the truth of this situation, I have tried to make careful and rather full studies of each of Albee's ten plays. By using a combination of *explication de texte* and Aristotelian part-whole analysis, I have aimed to give the reader as complete a sense of the play as it is possible for him to have without his actually reading it and seeing it in the theater—one of which I expect him to do. Stage history along with newspaper and periodical criticism of Albee's plays, because of its great volume, I have reluctantly had to excise from my manuscript. (I plan to publish some of this material separately later.) In the final chapter, however, I have very briefly evaluated the main lines taken by critics of each of Albee's plays.

I have not taken a position as an Albeephile nor as an Albeephobe. I have tried to be objective. My responsibilities to the reader I have viewed as involving a plea to him for an open mind and a fair hearing on behalf of a young playwright who quite possibly has opened on the American stage a door to a new and completely experimental kind of theater. Final judgment I leave to the reader.

I should like to express thanks to Dr. Walton Patrick and other colleagues of the Auburn University English Department for intellectual stimulation and suggestions. To Miss Sylvia E. Bowman, editor of the Twayne United States Authors Series, I once again find myself in special debt for kind consideration and patient counseling. To the librarians of the Ralph Brown Draughon Library at Auburn University and to those of the theater collection at the New York Public Library I am deeply grateful for help.

Finally, I acknowledge with thanks assistance provided by a research grant from the Auburn University Grant-in-Aid Fund.

RICHARD E. AMACHER

Auburn University

Contents

Preface

Chronology

1.	A Success Story	15
2.	Literary Theory and Views on Art	25
3.	Ancient Tragedy and Modern Absurdity	40
4.	Pity and Fear in Miniature	55
5.	Excursion into Naturalism	62
6.	Expressionistic Satire	75
7.	Battle of the Sexes—New Style	82
8.	Adaptations from Novels	109
9.	Experiment in Surrealism	130
10.	The Well-Made Play in the Theater of the Absurd	154
11.	Albee's Place in the Theater	165
	Notes and References	171
	Selected Bibliography	183
	Index	186

Chronology

1928 Edward Albee born March 12 in Washington, D. C. Adopted at age of two weeks by Reed and Frances Albee of Larchmont, N. Y. Named for his adopted grandfather, Edward Franklin Albee, part owner of the Keith-Albee Theater Circuit.

1940 Writes a three-act sex farce called *Aliqueen.*

1939-1949 Attends Rye Country Day School in Westchester County, New York; The Lawrenceville School at Lawrenceville, New Jersey; Valley Forge Military Academy, Wayne, Pennsylvania; and is graduated from The Choate School in Wallingford, Connecticut. Attends Trinity College, Hartford, Connecticut, for a year and a half.

1949-1958 Spends approximately a decade in Greenwich Village, living off a trust fund his maternal grandmother had left him in 1949 and supplementing it with earnings from various odd jobs.

1958 Writes *The Zoo Story.*

1959 First production of *The Zoo Story* in Berlin on September 28, at the *Schiller Theater Werkstatt.*

1960 American production of *The Zoo Story* at Provincetown Playhouse in Greenwich Village on January 14.

1960 *The Sandbox; Fam and Yam.*

1961 *The American Dream; Bartleby* (an operatic adaptation of Melville's short story), which fails; *The Death of Bessie Smith.*

1962 *Who's Afraid of Virginia Woolf?* First Broadway production, which wins Drama Critics' Award and other prizes.

1963 *The Ballad of the Sad Cafe,* an adaptation of Carson McCullers' novella.

1964 *Tiny Alice.*

1965 *Malcolm,* an adaptation of James Purdy's novel, fails.

1966 *A Delicate Balance,* which wins Pulitzer prize for drama.

1967 Receives honorary doctorate (Doctor of Literature) from Emerson College in Boston.

1967 *Everything in the Garden,* an adaptation of a play by Giles Cooper.

1968 *Box* and *Quotations from Chairman Mao Tse-tung.*

CHAPTER *1*

A Success Story

THE LIFE of Edward Albee reads like a Horatio Alger story. In the late nineteenth century the Alger heroes of *Ragged Dick, Tattered Tom, Luck and Pluck,* and *Sink or Swim*—all poor boys—inevitably rose to fame and wealth after struggling with tempation and poverty. Sometimes, to be sure, the presence of a rich benefactor facilitated their rise to fortune. Nevertheless, all these young heroes brilliantly exemplified the idea that virtue always receives an ultimate reward—preferably in cold cash. In the twentieth century, of course, everything is changed. And so we have an alteration in the saga of "the lucky orphan,"[1] as Albee has termed the history of his earliest years—a change to the fascinating and wonderfully ironic tale of rich boy makes good.

I "*The Lucky Orphan*"

Edward Albee was born in Washington, D. C., on March 12, 1928; and, at the age of two weeks, he was adopted by Reed A. and Frances Albee and brought to New York.[2] He was named for his adopted grandfather, Edward Franklin Albee, part owner of the Keith-Albee Theatre Circuit, a coast-to-coast chain of, at one time, over two hundred vaudeville theaters.[3] During 1928 Reed Albee retired from his father's theater business and took up "owning and showing three-and-five-gaited saddle horses."[4] This occupation apparently became his chief one until his death on August 2, 1961, in White Plains, New York. According to one obituary, he belonged to numerous clubs; according to another, his survivors included one other adopted child besides the playwright.[5] Albee's mother, Frances, a "former Bergdorf mannequin," who now lives in White Plains, impressed one interviewer as "a tall imperious suburban club lady" of "formidable" aspect.[6]

In these early years our "orphan" lived in a "sprawling Tudor stucco house in Westchester . . . a world of servants, tutors, riding lessons; winters in Miami [or Palm Beach], summers sailing on the Sound. There was a Rolls to bring him, snuggled in lap robes, to matinées in the city; an inexhaustible wardrobe housed in a closet big as an ordinary room; a profusion of toys; numberless pets, ranging from a St. Bernard to pull his sleigh in the wintertime to a penful of guinea pigs."[7]

As a child, Edward Albee frequently found himself in the midst of theater people—Ed Wynn, Jimmy Durante, and Walter Pidgeon—who "drifted in and out of the mansion" at Larchmont, where he then lived.[8] At about this time he began seeing shows—the first he recalls being *Jumbo,* a spectacle—and he also started writing poetry.[9] At the age of twelve, he wrote his first play, a three-act sex-farce entitled *Aliqueen.*[10]

II *In and Out of School*

Formal education, meanwhile, had begun to present difficulties. Because his parents often spent their winters in places like Florida and Arizona, a good deal of transplanting ensued. Albee claims that he had little chance to learn anything because he was always being uprooted from school.[11] Boarding school, which he started when eleven, after attending the Rye Country Day School, only continued the same erratic pattern instead of remedying it. "Albee took the Holden Caulfield route through formal education," according to one writer; for he was "kicked out" of Lawrenceville preparatory school (for "cutting" classes) and Valley Forge Military Academy; he finally was graduated from Choate; and then he was dismissed from Trinity College in his sophomore year, reportedly for failure to attend Chapel and certain classes.[12]

Faint sparks of hope, however, now and then illuminated Albee's hectic career through the long, dark valley of adolescence. One of his poems saw publication in *Kaleidoscope,* a Texas magazine.[13] At the age of seventeen, in a work entitled "Nihilist," he had written some lines that prophesied his later rebellion: "What causes him to mouth the purple grape/Of life experience, then spit the seeds/Back at the world?"[14] Then, too, his English teacher at Choate "remembers sitting hour after hour

... with him, reading his many, big, hand-filled pages." "One night," he says, "I was faced with fifty of them."

The director of admissions at Choate had predicted that Albee would "distinguish himself in literature."[15] But we hope that this prediction did not rest on the evidence of Albee's long one-act melodrama, well-stuffed with clichés and called *Schism,* that appeared in the Choate *Literary Magazine.*[16] After he left Choate to take up his brief residence at Trinity College, he learned a little more about the practical end of the drama by turning from his role of playwright to that of actor in Maxwell Anderson's *The Masque of Kings.* He played the part of Emperor Franz Joseph.[17]

III *"The Richest Boy in Greenwich Village"*

After Trinity College, Albee faced the prospect of earning his own living. Against the wishes of his foster parents, he left home in 1950 intent upon following a career as a writer.[18] The perils of such an undertaking, although considerably lessened by a hundred-thousand-dollar trust fund his grandmother had set up for him in 1949, must have seemed very real to him. According to the terms of the trust, he received about fifty dollars a week from his twenty-first until his thirtieth birthday, when he obtained full possession of the big money.[19] Any degree of financial independence greatly strengthens the hand of a writer, particularly a young one; for it means he is free to devote himself to his art. Yet Albee found life in Manhattan expensive enough to necessitate his sharing a Greenwich Village apartment and his taking a series of odd jobs to supplement his regular income. Considering the early background of our "lucky orphan" and the fact that he was still "probably the richest boy in Greenwich Village," this kind of "slumming" must have made him feel that he was at last living like a grown-up.[20] Although many young writers have acquired valuable experience through this same odd-job route, few have inherited so wealthy and so generous a grandmother.

During the "blank" decade between the time he left Trinity College and the date of his first produced play, *The Zoo Story,* Albee worked at various odd jobs. For about a year before he left home, he wrote music programs for radio station WNYC. He also worked as an office boy for Warwick and Legler, an advertising agency. At Bloomingdale's he sold records; at Schirmer's, books. At the luncheonette of the Manhattan Towers Hotel he faced the public as a counterman.[21] Having a flair for walking, he joined the ranks of Western Union (1955–58) and saw Manhattan—on foot. He liked this job, he admits, because "it got me out into the air."[22] According to some gentlemen of the press, he delivered death notices.[23] If this anecdote is true, he had ample opportunity to study human nature in its most trying moment.

During this period he changed his dwelling place several times. "I've lived in a lot of places," he told one interviewer, "—a fifteen-dollar-a-month cold-water flat on the lower East Side, a great big loft right in the middle of the garment district, for seventy a month, and a couple of other places in the village."[24] One reporter mentions a loft at Seventh Avenue and Twenty-Seventh Street, a six-floor walk-up on Mulberry Street, and a place on Henry Street. This same writer describes these sundry habitations and odd jobs as constituting for Albee "an era the very odor of which permeates the life and lines of Jerry the lonely psychotic in 'The Zoo Story'."[25] Albee himself has characterized this period as his "peddling years": "My personal drift corresponded with a time when the country was in the middle of a drift."[26]

But William Flanagan, who roomed with Albee during nine years of this "village decade," tells a different story. A good deal of nonsense has been printed about Albee's village decade, according to Flanagan. "Curiously enough, its most characteristic segment was passed in an airy, comfortable and altogether proper floor-through flat in Chelsea." And, says Flanagan, he has always found it difficult to decide (from what the press has published about Albee) whether Albee was being represented as a "Bohemian *poseur*" or an obscure, insecure poverty-ridden poet.

Somewhere between these two extremes, Flanagan suggests, the truth lies: "He was, to be sure, adrift and like most of the rest of us, he had arrived in town with an unsown wild oat or two. But from the beginning he was, in his outwardly impassive way, determined to write.... He adored the theatre from the beginning and there can't have been anything of even mild importance that we didn't see together...." At that time, Flanagan continues, Albee displayed an "unyielding" and "thoroughly unfashionable admiration for the work of Tennessee Williams."[27]

IV *The Successful Young Dramatist*

Some years earlier, in 1953, on the advice and encouragement of Thornton Wilder, then at the MacDowell Colony in Peterborough, New Hampshire, Albee had turned his thoughts from poetizing to playwriting;[28] but little evidence came forth during this decade of any publishable writings. Quite dramatically, however, just before his thirtieth birthday in 1958, when he was "desperate" and when it had begun to look as if he "wouldn't make it," he sat down to "a wobbly table in the kitchen" and typed out *The Zoo Story*.[29]

The history of the production of this play owes much to Albee's friend, William Flanagan, who sent it to David Diamond in Florence, Italy, who passed it on to Pinkas Braun, an actor in Zurich, who referred it to Mrs. Stefani Hunzinger, director of the dramatic department of a large German publishing firm, S. Fischer, in Frankfurt.[30] Eventually, Boleslaw Barlog produced it at the Schiller Theater *Werkstatt* in Berlin on September 28, 1959, along with Samuel Beckett's *Krapp's Last Tape*. Albee, who flew to Germany for the production, didn't understand a word of the German translation. Later, the play appeared in twelve other German cities; and it finally was presented in Greenwich Village at the Off-Broadway Provincetown Playhouse on January 14, 1960; there, under a "Theatre 1960" billing, it marked the beginning of his rise as the King of Off-Broadway.[31] In the Off-Broadway notices for this year Henry Hewes noted the promise of "another new writer, Edward Albee."[32]

Albee's good fortune in early associating himself with Richard Barr and Clinton Wilder, two young producers willing to gamble on a change in the climate of the American theater, cannot be too much stressed.[33] His choice of Alan Schneider as his director also showed, if anything, even more acumen. Theater people who have worked with Albee agree, in turn, "that he has enormous talent and a complete professionalism."[34]

Like Eugene O'Neill, Albee knows the theater inside out. He directed the Producer Theater production of *The Sandbox*, his third play, at the Cherry Lane Theater in 1962. This particular season amounted to a real campaign on Albee's part in behalf of "the theater of the absurd"; for at this time, along with Barr and Wilder, he undertook the production of nine plays for a total of fifty-five performances, including (besides *The Sandbox*) his own *The Zoo Story* (directed by Barr) and *The American Dream* (directed by Schneider), such works as Jean Genet's *Deathwatch,* Jack Richardson's *Gallows Humor,* Fernando Arrabal's *Picnic on the Battlefield,* Eugene Ionesco's *The Killer,* Samuel Beckett's *Endgame* and Kenneth Koch's *Bertha.*[35]

In conjunction with Barr and Wilder, Albee two years later was still plugging hard his penchant for the "absurd" with a group called "Theater 1964," located at the Cherry Lane Theater, and doing such works as Beckett's *Play* and Harold Pinter's *The Lover.* In addition, by reinvesting in the project part of the profits from *Who's Afraid of Virginia Woolf?,* he had founded a new American playwright "school" that supported the early work of less well-known figures like LeRoi Jones, Lawrence Osgood, Harvey Perr, Howard Sackler, and Lee Kalcheim among others.[36]

In these and similar activities—notably the Broadway production of *Who's Afraid of Virginia Woolf?, The Ballad of the Sad Cafe,* and *Tiny Alice*—Albee has emerged as the leader of the American wing of the "theater of the absurd." There can be little doubt that, although yet a young man, he has already made such a deep—and probably lasting—wound on the traditional Broadway-Hollywood theater that his name will go down in history.[37]

The effect of premature fame on a young dramatist might well prove very damaging to his creative growth. More than one news writer said as much in print on the occasion of Albee's being "fluttered over by all the reviewers"—even before the tumultuous success of *Virginia Woolf.*[38] But while *The Ballad of the Sad Cafe* and *Tiny Alice* enjoyed less long runs than *Virginia Woolf,* they indicated no diminution of their author's artistic ability. In fact, we might argue that both these later plays show Albee attempting progressively more difficult problems in the theater, ones demanding increasingly greater skill.

William Flanagan, who probably knows Albee as well as anybody, has written that "no one who really knows the man [Albee] is in anything but awe of his uncanny coolness, his ability to view his own spectacular success with detachment, humor, and a shrewd estimation of the limitations and shortcomings of his work to date."[39] At the same time, Flanagan refers to Albee as a "chronically ambivalent man"; and he adds that "Edward . . . is widely reputed to be a mysterious number."[40] Beyond this somewhat ambiguous statement, little more seems pertinent to our discussion except Albee's liking for walking, bowling, books, music, modern painting, Pekingese dogs, and two or three cats.[41]

V *Lecturer, at Home and Abroad*

As a lecturer, Albee has appeared both at home and abroad on many collegiate and other platforms. He spoke, and was well-received, at the New York Writers Conference held at Wagner College on Staten Island (July 17–19, 1960). A clipping (June 14, 1961) in the theater collection of the New York Public Library lists Albee as having accepted an invitation to make a good-will tour of South America with the New York Repertory and to lecture at the University of Buenos Aires. Another clipping announces his teaching at a playwriting workshop at the Circle in the Square Theater School. The New York *World Telegram and Sun* for May 3, 1962, stated that he had received a grant of one thousand dollars from Washington and Lee University at Lexington, Virginia, to act as Glasgow Visiting Professor there. On April 19–21, 1963, Albee starred in an open quarrel with the producer Robert Whitehead at the famous Princeton Response Weekend symposium on the arts, sponsored by *Esquire* magazine. *The Village Voice* of December 13, 1962, carried a note to the effect that Albee would discuss "The American Imagination" at eight-thirty on Wednesday evening, December 19, in Columbia University Harkness Theater. On May 6 of the same year he shared the platform with John Ciardi and Max Lerner at Hofstra College.

At about this time, Mary Lukas noted in *Show* (February, 1963) that Albee had become "a responsible member of the intellectual community, participating in learned panels and lectures in half a dozen schools" (83). On February 10, 1963, he appeared at the YM-YWHA poetry center, along with Arthur Kopit, Alan Schneider, Robert Brustein, Alan Pryce-Jones, and John Simon. And these are only a few of his numerous engagements as lecturer, which helped to keep him in the public eye. *International Who's Who* carried his name for the first time in the 1962–63 issue.

The 1963–64 theater season marked the greatest growth of Albee's popularity. Four of his plays ran more or less concurrently during this single season: *Who's Afraid of Virginia Woolf?* closed after 663 performances; *The Ballad of the Sad Cafe,* after 124; *The American Dream* and *The Zoo Story,* running on the same bill, enjoyed a revival of 143 performances. Albee had definitely "arrived" in the theater, and he was in greater demand than ever as guest lecturer.

On the international circuit, apropos the success of *Virginia Woolf* in translation at such places as Hamburg and Belgrade, Albee spent four weeks in the Soviet Union, lecturing under the auspices of the American State Department. He visited Leningrad, Odessa, Kiev, and Moscow. When he talked with the poet Yevtushenko in the latter's home and also with several other Russian writers, he found them "isolated"—"not depressed and not optimistic—but ironic."[42] The Russians had considered producing *The Death of Bessie Smith,* but apparently had received little encouragement from Albee. Later in New York, he said that he had had misgivings about a Russian production of this particular play because the "attacks on some aspects of American society in 1937" in the play might be misconstrued by the Russians as an indictment of American society now. Albee and John Steinbeck, who nominated him for the tour, left Russia abruptly to protest the Soviet Union's retaliatory arrest in November, 1963, of Professor F. C. Barghoorn, head of Soviet studies at Yale University.

Previously, during this two-month tour of mainly Socialist countries, Albee has also visited Hungary, Czechoslovakia, and Poland. In Warsaw he attended each evening one of the theaters of the Polish capital. "He also discussed contemporary drama with the editors of 'Dialog'—the [Polish] monthly magazine," and he met and talked with students of the English Department at Warsaw University.[43]

VI *Fame and Fortune*

In the summer of 1964 Albee visited Italy, further establishing his already widespread reputation there as an international playwright. Besides his earlier visit to Florence in 1952, Albee had also flown to Rome on December 27, 1962, for a ten-day conference about the production of *Who's Afraid of Virginia Woolf?* with director Franco Zeffirelli and actor Marcello Mastroianni.

A Success Story

Largely because he represents the American counterpart of the main thrust of the modern European theater, Albee has, from the first appearance of *The Zoo Story* in 1959, enjoyed wide acclaim in Continental centers of the drama. In Germany, particularly, I found, during my Fulbright professorship at the *Englisches Seminar* of Würzburg University (1961–62), more interest in Albee than in any other American playwright. Thornton Wilder, Tennessee Williams, Eugene O'Neill, and Arthur Miller, all highly popular elsewhere in Germany, were possibly better known; but they did not excite the students so much as Albee. The air rang with talk of the "absurd"; and the new, imaginative experiments of Ionesco, Genet, and Beckett had captured audiences of both provincial towns and cosmopolitan centers. The satire and annihilating social criticisms of Albee and the Continental "absurdists," allied with their strong imaginative flair, appealed strongly to the Germans and other Europeans who were looking for a new order of social and religious values. These people did not resent the destruction of much that they knew was false; and, it seemed to me, they rather welcomed the advent of a playwright who could represent a genuinely self-critical attitude on the part of postwar Americans toward their institutions and culture.

As American spokesman for this new movement that so deeply challenges the "establishment," Albee has already won several prizes. Quoted in the *New York Times* of June 30, 1961, as angry because Off-Broadway never received consideration at play-award time, Albee failed to make sense. For he himself had only shortly before received the Lola d'Annunzio prize for "sustained accomplishments in original playwriting" in *The Death of Bessie Smith* and in *The American Dream*, both of which were then playing at the Cherry Lane Theater.[44] He had, moreover, but a year earlier in May, 1960, conferred upon him the Vernon Rice Award for outstanding achievement in an Off-Broadway production. Moreover, *The Village Voice* had given him its "Obie" award for *The Zoo Story*. The Foreign Press Association Award during 1960–61 went to him for *The Death of Bessie Smith* and for *The American Dream*. In 1963 he again won this award, becoming the first two-time winner in the history of this prize. He received the Best Foreign Play Award of 1962 in Buenos Aires in September, 1962.

But on Broadway fame and fortune also awaited him. *Who's Afraid of Virginia Woolf?* marked the peak thus far of his popularity and success. It captured five Antoinette Perry Awards for such matters as directing and acting; the already mentioned Foreign Press Association Award; and similar prizes from the New York Drama Critics, the Outer Circle, the American Theater Wing, and the American National Theater and Academy.[45] Later, when the Board of Trustees of Columbia University refused to award him the Pulitzer Prize for *Virginia Woolf* and when drama critic John Mason Brown and Professor John Gassner of Yale, two members of the selecting jury, resigned in protest against the narrow-minded considerations of the trustees, Albee found himself more than ever in the limelight of controversy.[46] According to the *New York Times* of March 5, 1964, the movie rights to *Virginia Woolf* finally sold to Warner Brothers for approximately five hundred thousand dollars. When asked why he gave up *Virginia Woolf* to the movies—earlier he had intimated he might not—Albee replied, "A combination of greed and fatigue."[47]

VII *Albee Today*

Today popular interest in Edward Albee continues, despite one outright failure and relatively short runs of his other five plays since *Virginia Woolf*. Few would deny his appeal to both "uptown" and "downtown" audiences, Broadway and Off-Broadway; and he remains, in his late thirties, possibly the most thought-provoking, serious dramatist at work in America at the present moment. Commuting, as he does between his Village apartment on West Tenth Street and his summer home at Montauk on Long Island, he sometimes feels a certain sense of removal from the way most Americans live. Specifically, he objects to "a certain complacence" in the American character: "a very comfortable feeling that there's not really any point in doing anything except sitting back and watching television"[48]—the hypnosis which paralyzes the kind of responsible and intelligible action that in the past has made our country a watchword for something other than drift, inaction, and ugly Americanism. And closely associated with this criticism is Albee's view of the state of the theater.

CHAPTER 2

Literary Theory and Views on Art

I *Broadway and Hollywood*

THE HEALTH of a nation, a society, can be determined by the art it demands."[1] With this statement Albee sounds loudly and clearly his attack on the existing—barely existing—American theater as represented by its two major establishments, Broadway and Hollywood. These two withering limbs of the entertainment world on this side of the Atlantic have, along with television, desecrated almost all the values of the drama. Briefly, the stage has a high degree of technological perfection and expenditure in such matters as photography, direction, acting, music, lighting and sound effects; but the play itself is often stereotyped and sentimental in plot, character, and theme.

A vast difference exists between the United States and places like West Berlin, which Albee calls his "second home town," because he received his first real recognition there, or like Buenos Aires, which he says has one hundred experimental theaters.[2] Broadway demands an established money-maker; and, as everyone knows, the demands of art and high finance often conflict. Essentially, the Broadway theater is "absurd" in the sense that it is ridiculous. Albee describes this situation when he says

> What . . . could be more absurd than a theatre in which the esthetic criterion is something like this: A "good" play is one which makes money; a "bad" play (in the sense of "Naughty! Naughty!" I guess) is one which does not; a theatre in which playwrights are encouraged (what a funny word!) to think of themselves as little cogs in a great big wheel; a theatre in which imitation has given way to imitation of imitation; a theatre in which London "hits" are, willy nilly, in a kind of reverse of chauvinism, greeted in a manner not unlike a colony's obeisance to the Crown; a theatre in which real estate owners and theatre

> party managements predetermine the success of unknown quantities; a theatre in which everybody scratches and bites for billing as though it meant access to the last bomb shelter on earth; a theatre in which, in a given season, there was not a single performance of a play by Beckett, Brecht, Chekhov, Genet, Ibsen, O'Casey, Pirandello, Shaw, Strindberg—or Shakespeare? What . . . could be more absurd than that?[3]

But the public must take some share of the blame: "A lazy public . . . produces a slothful and irresponsible theatre." Theatergoers must "get up off their six-ninety seats and find out what the theatre is *really* about."[4] Although Albee's plays have enjoyed truly amazing financial success, he has insisted that he is more "concerned about the state of our theatre culture, and the directions in which our theatre will be allowed to move. . . . I am more pleased by the rewards of the theatre as a creative environment than I am with its immediate rewards, and . . . if I thought the theatre would be a better place without TINY ALICE, I would close it tomorrow."[5]

II Fam and Yam

Another aspect of this indictment of the Broadway-Hollywood, financial-success establishment occurs in Albee's little known play *Fam and Yam,* which appeared with Samuel Beckett's *Embers* and Harry Tierney's *Nekros* on a special triple bill of the Greater New York Chapter of ANTA's Matinee Theatre Series (February 18, 1963) at the Theatre de Lys in New York. Designated variously as "a satirical interview between a famous American playwright who resembled William Inge, and a young American playwright who resembled Mr. Albee," as "a comic dialogue between playwrights," and as "a light-hearted dialogue that demonstrates its author's ability to laugh at himself," *Fam and Yam* actually discloses in yet another form Albee's sense of the conflict between Broadway and Off-Broadway.[6]

A one-act, or rather a one-scene, play, *Fam and Yam* presents an interview between two American playwrights, an older famous one, Fam, and a younger one, Yam. Yam is described in the brief preface as "*an intense, bony young man, whose crew cut is in need of a trim*"; he is equipped with "*sweat socks, an overlong scarf, an old issue of Evergreen Review under one arm.*"[7] The older man, Fam, is "*a no-longer thin gentleman, a year or so either side of fifty,"* who looks like *"a slightly rumpled account executive"* or like *"a faintly foppish Professor of History."*[8] The action takes place in Fam's East Side apartment, presumably in New York, which is decorated with expensive original paintings—one Braque, two Modiglianis, one Motherwell, and a Klein. The apartment has *"a view of the bridge,"* a plum-colored sofa, and white walls.[9] During the interview, Fam's main interest is the sherry bottle.

Yam had apparently ingratiated himself into Fam's attention by a flattering letter asking for the interview. Evidently the letter had named Miller, Williams, Wilder, and Inge as "right up there."[10] The naming of Inge is especially pointed, and the effect is that of the younger man's envy of the older, established playwrights. But, envious as he is of Fam's good fortune, Yam does not hide his consciousness that Fam is "a real pro," which, according to a nameless professor at Columbia University, is only another name for a "high-class hack."[11] While Yam says he does not agree with this verdict, he nevertheless suggests that "a continued popular acceptance of a man's work . . ." does something rather disturbing to a writer's integrity.[12] Fam talks platitudes, remarkably like the character Peter in *The Zoo Story*.

The whole dialogue, in fact, so much resembles this latter play that it sounds as if Albee were writing according to a formula—interesting and aggressive underdog bites helpless Mr. Dry-as-Dust. In the following speech of Fam, it is not difficult to find Albee's feeling that the older establishment of dramatists, represented by Inge and the others, may soon be a thing of the past: "The new generation's knocking at the door. Gelber, Richardson, Kopit . . . (*Shrugs*) . . . you . . . (*mock woe.*) You youngsters are going to push us out of the way. . . ."[13] The reference to Yam (who resembles Albee) is as pointed as the other, earlier one had been to Inge.

After Fam pours himself another sherry, Yam, who gets down to the business of the interview, tells him in an aggressive manner about what he plans to put in print; and Fam, who is by now helping himself to his fourth and fifth sherry, becomes "a little tipsy." As a result, he echoes, repeats, and agrees to everything Yam says he is going to include in the printed interview—for example, that theater owners, producers, backers of plays, unions, critics, directors, and even "theatre parties" are all "villains."[14] This attack mounts to a climax when Yam says he plans to refer to "hit-happy theatre owners" as "ignorant, greedy real-estate owners"; to producers as "opportunistic, out-for-a-buck businessmen, masquerading as . . ."; to playwrights as "nothing better than businessmen themselves . . . you know . . . out for the loot . . . just as cynically as anyone else"; to directors as "slick, sleight-of-hand artists . . . talking all noble and uncompromising *until* they get into rehearsal . . . and *then* . . ."; to the critics as setting themselves up as "sociological arbiters . . . misusing their function"; and to "theatre parties" (see above) as "pinheads."[15] Fam, who thinks this attack very funny, laughs uproariously. The parallel between this part of the play and the scene in *The Zoo Story* in which Jerry tickles Peter is inescapable.

When Yam leaves, Fam does not take his hand, his own hands being full of the bottle and the glass—his sixth sherry. Only after Yam has gone does Fam sufficiently sober to realize that the young man really intends writing and printing exactly what he had said he would during the interview. And even this shocker occurs to him only after the phone rings, and Yam thanks him for the interview. "The Interview?" Fam gasps; and he repeats the word while one of the two Modiglianis "*frowns*," the Braque "*peels*," the Klein "*tilts*," the Motherwell comes crashing to the floor, and the curtain falls.[16] Ironically, the title of the interview, according to Yam, was to have been "In Search of a Hero."[17] Fam argues, however, that if everybody connected with the theater is in the "villain" class, as Yam maintains, then there is no room left for a hero. "That's just the point!" Yam replies. "Everybody's culpable."

We must not, as some have done, too hastily dismiss Albee's seven-page *Fam and Yam* as a mere bagatelle. For it poses a serious, ringing challenge to the dull establishment we have accustomed ourselves to calling "the American theater." That Inge, Miller, Williams, and Wilder have not brought lawsuits against Albee may indicate their recognition of the truth of his charge. Or it could mean that they think the shoe does not fit them.

III *Audience and Critic*

Albee has made much in his press interviews and in his television appearances of the fact that the critic-led, sheeplike audience of the American newspaper and magazine world may be largely responsible for the situation outlined in *Fam and Yam.* "We hear so often of the responsibility of the artist to his audience, but far too little is ever said about the responsibility of an audience—of a society, if you will—to the people who fashion its entertainments." Albee speaks of "a roundabout of misunderstanding between the critic and the audience" in which the critic "believes it to be his responsibility, his function, to reflect what he considers to be the taste of his readers . . . and the reader—the audience—has come to the no less lamentable conclusion that a play review [by the critic] he reads, does, indeed, reflect his taste."

"It would be a laughable game of blind man's bluff," he continues, "if the implications were not so melancholy . . . if the damage done to the theatre as an art form as well as an entertainment medium were not so cruel." Because the critic is such a powerful force, "the audience tends to take the critic on face value"; therefore,

> . . . the critic might do well to face up to the responsibilities of his awesome power. It is the responsibility of the critic not only to inform the public what has occurred by its present standards, but, as well, to inform the public taste. It is not enough for a critic to tell his audience how well a play succeeds in its intention; he must also judge that intention by the absolute standards of the theatre as an art form. The point is easily made. The Broadway theatres that are full each night are full at entertainments that succeed entirely in their intentions, even though these intentions are relatively low on any absolute scale. It is far easier for a play that attempts the point of twenty on a graph of one hundred to achieve the point of nineteen than for a play that attempts eighty to reach even forty. But we all know that forty is higher than nineteen. Yet, at the end of each season, the critics in their summary pieces lament the lack of serious and ambitious plays on the boards. But the odd thing is that these same critics have spent the season urging their readers to rush to the nineteen point plays. The audience is led to believe that these are better plays. Well, perhaps they are better plays *to* their audience, but they are not better plays *for* the audience. And since the critic fashions the audience taste, whether he intends to or not, he succeeds, each season, in merely lowering it.

In Albee's sometimes less-than-merry war with the critics, he accuses Walter Kerr of determining the excellence of a play on grounds of "its immediate mass appeal." To "carry Mr. Kerr's idea to its logical and dank end" means judging Ferde Grofé's *Grand Canyon Suite* as superior to Beethoven's last quartet. According to this criterion,

> Norman Rockwell is a better painter than Soutine; CAROUSEL a better piece of musical theatre than WOZZECK; FOREVER AMBER a finer book than REMEMBRANCE OF THINGS PAST. But the contrary is true, as Mr. Kerr knows, as we all know. The final determination of the value of a work of art is the opinion of an informed and educated people over a long period of time. It may well be true that a tree which falls in the forest with no one to hear it, makes no sound; but the crucial point is that it can matter only to people who have been taught the difference between a sapling and a weed.

Most of these views of Albee originated in an interview, held in the Billy Rose Theater, concerning a rumor that *Tiny Alice* was about to close and following the mixed critical reception that had greeted this play.

Of his plays, Albee admits that they "... are imperfect, I'm rather happy to say—it leaves me something to do, and there may be flaws in the production as well, but I suspect—and I am not paranoid yet, because I haven't been in the playwriting business very long—I suspect that there are many, many people who have been intimidated into either not understanding TINY ALICE or not taking the trouble to see for themselves if they *would* understand it for no better reason than that they have been told they would not."

In completing his remarks on the responsibilities of audience and critics to create a better theater, Albee makes a plea for a fair hearing of *Tiny Alice* and asks the great American audience "if it really wants as little from the theatre as those critics who believe they reflect its taste would have it believe."[18] "In the final analysis," of course, "society gets the kind of theatre it deserves."[19] During the Princeton University seminar, Albee, in drawing attention to what he called "the mindless dictatorship of the audience," contrasted the low-class demands of the American entertainment establishment and its dictatorship from the bottom with Soviet bureaucratic dictatorship from the top (apropos Yevtushenko's not being permitted to attend the Princeton seminar). He qualified this statement, however, by adding that "The American audience can have any kind of theatre it wants. . . ."[20]

This whole problem of the joint responsibility of the audience-writer-critic team in creating an artistically satisfying theater exhibits many facets; and one rather important one is how the audience will react to a so-called difficult play, like, for example, *Tiny Alice.* At this point Albee was quick to indicate that "no two works of art are of the same density" and that "the true worth of a work" cannot be "determined by its simplicity, by the ease with which its content can be weighed": "A book that you read only once, a play that leaves you as quickly as you leave it, may have value as diversion and may, as well, be very skillfully done—had better be, in fact—but works of that sort tend to reap greater immediate rewards for their creators than they do lasting one for their audiences."

A work that is "difficult, or confusing, or elusive" is not, however, necessarily better than a simpler one. "But the truth is that art isn't easy; it isn't easy for its perpetrators, and it demands of its audience the willingness to bring to it some of the intensity and perception its creators put into it." In the last analysis, however, "if an author's work can not speak clearly for itself, then no length of clarification by the author as to his intention will make the work of art in question—if, indeed, it is a work of art to begin with—any less opaque, any less faulty."[21]

Alan Schneider, Albee's favorite director, once stated that "the theater is always for the happy few. It is not an art for the many." When Schneider made this statement, Albee concurred, reiterating his view that, until the audiences lived up to their responsibility, the theater would of necessity be "for the few."[22]

IV *The Theater of the Absurd*

Somewhat amusingly, Albee tells us that the first time he heard that he was a member of "the theater of the absurd," he was offended; for he thought it applied to the standard, inane Broadway fare.[23] The purpose of the genuine "theater of the absurd," as Albee sees it, is "to make a man face up to the human condition as it really is. . . ."[24] Granting that Albee may have come to this idea independently, we must point out that Martin

Esslin had said in print substantially the same thing about a year before.

According to Esslin, the "theater of the absurd" "does not reflect despair or a return to dark irrational forces but expresses modern man's endeavor to come to terms with the world in which he lives. It attempts to make him face up to the human condition as it really is, to free him from illusions that are bound to cause constant maladjustment and disappointment. . . . For the dignity of man lies in his ability to face reality in all its senselessness; to accept it freely, without fear, without illusions—and to laugh at it."[25]

With this definition of Esslin, we may compare Albee's: "The Theatre of the Absurd is an absorption-in-art of certain existentialist and post-existentialist philosophical concepts having to do, in the main, with man's attempt to make sense for himself out of his senseless position in a world which makes no sense—which makes no sense because the moral, religious, political and social structures man has erected to "illusion" himself have collapsed.[26] Albee quotes from Camus, Ionesco, and Esslin to support these ideas.

In February, 1962, he alluded to The Theatre of the Absurd Repertory Company as "currently playing at New York's Off-Broadway Cherry Lane Theatre—presenting works by Beckett, Ionesco, Genet, Arrabal, Jack Richardson, Kenneth Koch and myself—being the first such collective representation of the movement in the United States. . . ." Quick to deny imitation or servile following of his obviously European sources, Albee insists that "The Theatre of the Absurd represent[s] a group only in the sense that they seem to be doing something of the same thing in vaguely similar ways at approximately the same time. . . .[27] Albee's own work and that of his European predecessors—theorists as well as dramatists—often bear more than vague resemblance to one another.

If the French avant-garde had any viability at all in the American theater of the early 1960's, it manifested it through the early Social Realism of Albee's plays such as *The Zoo Story, The Sandbox, The Death of Bessie Smith,* and *The American Dream* rather than through the more Existentialist dramas of Sartre, Camus, and Beckett. Albee shows understanding and insight into the history of American drama as a whole when he declares that "It is my guess that the theatre in the United States will always hew more closely to the post-Ibsen-Chekhov tradition than does the theatre in France, let us say. It is our nature as a country, a society. But we will experiment. . . ."[28] He implies that the "theater of the absurd" has permanently and irretrievably changed the direction of the history of the drama, as French Impressionism changed the history of painting.

Pleading for a fair hearing of the new plays, he wrote, early in 1962, that "The avant-garde theatre is fun; it is free-swinging, bold, iconoclastic and often wildly, wildly funny. If you will approach it with childlike innocence—putting your standard responses aside . . . if you will approach it on its own terms, I think you will be in for a liberating surprise."[29] Then he added, "You will not only be doing yourself some good, but you will be having a great time, to boot."

The extent of Albee's commitment to this movement may be seen as it affects his review, which *The Village Voice* printed on July 11, 1963, of Lillian Ross's novel, *Vertical and Horizontal.* Two paragraphs of his conclusion show the affinity of his mind for socially critical yet basically absurdist material:

> The whole book . . . is an attack on the school of analysis . . . [which] would adjust a man to his society without first relating him to himself. It is a terrifying examination of the living death, the pseudo-involved cliché-ridden mindless living death that passes for existing in our vast middle-class society. It is also a very funny book.
>
> Oh, most of the humor is dark and sad and deeply troubling, and forces one to view horror and absurdity and futility with the double sight of great laughter and great pity, but a lot of it is just plain funny even while the wit is always more than a little acerbic.[30]

V *Art and Reality*

In the twentieth century, possibly because of the alarming acceleration of knowledge about the physical, or astronomical, universe and about the nature and extent of matter—as well as the suspicion that philosophy and religion have to some extent been based in the past upon ignorance of these matters—the question about the nature of reality looms large. And, since art and reality seem to be at the same time independent and interrelatedly dependent, the lines of demarcation have puzzled many theorists on art.

"It's not the purpose of any art form to be just like life," Albee explains. "Reality on stage is highly selective reality, chosen to give form. Real dialogue on stage is impossible. . . . Make a tape recording of people and try to put that on stage."[31] Many modern dramatists like to believe that, when they reach a certain point in their compositions, the characters become real enough to "take over the situation" and to talk and act like real people. According to Albee, every writer worth his salt must start with a "fairly general idea" about where he is going.[32] Unlike the Existentialists who start with the proposition that man exists, that we *know* that we exist, Albee is willing to entertain, perhaps only facetiously, a doubt as to even this starting point:

> What happens in my plays is, I think, an accurate mirror of reality. There's always a certain amount of selection and hyperbole in art, but not so much that what I say is less than true. What people object to in my plays is a certain objectivity. I suffer for my subjects, of course, but I do not slop over into sentimentality. Everything must be measured against something else, I feel, to be understood. One enlarges the canvas to see what the separate elements mean. I have a faculty for objectivity even in my own life. Half the time I find my own rages and anxieties quite funny . . . . . Maybe . . . I don't exist at all.[33]

VI *The Offensive Playwright*

Because Albee does attempt a more difficult, a more deeply penetrating, view of reality than some of the older dramatists, who by comparison seem merely to scratch the surface of illusion, Albee has earned for himself all kinds of opprobrious epithets from holders of orthodox social, political, and theological opinions, as well as from drama critics bent on preserving the status quo. Consequently, we find him defending his position by saying that the playwright should not only entertain but also criticize society, should not only criticize society but also deliberately offend it—and intentionally do so.[34]

Social complacency is, as has already been indicated, surely one of Albee's main targets:

> Is the play offensive [he asks of his satire *The American Dream*]: I certainly hope so; it is my intention to offend—as well as to amuse and entertain. Is it nihilistic, immoral, defeatist? . . . let me answer that [it] is a picture of our time—as I see it, of course. Every honest work is a personal, private yowl, a statement of one's individual pleasure and pain; but I hope that The American Dream is something more than that. I hope it transcends the personal and private, and has something to do with the anguish of us all.[35]

Two fairly similar statements he made about this same play, possibly his strongest one in regard to social criticism, show that he means business. It is, he says, "an examination of the American Scene, an attack on the substitution of artificial for real values in our society, a condemnation of complacent cruelty, emasculation and vacuity; it is a stand against the fiction that everything in this slipping land of ours is peachy-keen."[36] Or "It's about the substitution of artificial values for real values in American society, the shameful treatment of old people and a symbolic and at the same time actual murder."[37]

In an eloquent rejoinder to Joseph Hayes's defense of the status quo theater as "a dream place of escape and never an arena of involvement," a place where pat answers must be given "by the fall of the third-act curtain," Albee writes—in connection with *Virginia Woolf*—

> Well, if the theater must bring us only what we can immediately apprehend or comfortably relate to, let us stop going to the theater entirely; let us play patty-cake with one another, or sit in our rooms and contemplate our paunchy middles.
>
> Further: If the theater must only, as Mr. Hayes puts it, "reflect or express the fundamental beliefs, feelings, convictions, aspirations" of our audiences, then, say I, down with all debate; down with all playwrights who have questioned the underpinnings of all the fundamental beliefs, etc.; down with all the playwrights who have not been content merely to reassure their audiences that all their values were dandy; down, then, say I, with Molière, Ibsen, Shaw, Aristophanes. Down with the theater as an educational as well as an entertainment medium. Down with the theater as a force for social and political advancement. Down with the theater! And up with the Fascism of a theater dedicated to satisfying only the whimperings of a most unworthy audience.[38]

VII *Favorite Playwrights*

One approach to understanding Albee's theories of the drama leads down the avenue of his favorite playwrights. That he likes Noel Coward we find a little surprising, for Coward fails to understand the avant-garde and has said so publicly. Albee has taken him to task for this failure: "Noel Coward can be a bore," he writes. "He bores his admirers every time he gets within earshot of a reporter by announcing how old-fashioned a writer he is, how the theatre has left him behind, how he does not understand the . . . 'avant-garde' playwrights of today, feels no sympathy with them." He would remind Coward that "the theatre goes in many directions simultaneously" and that, difficult as it is to understand, Coward has similar "preoccupations" with Beckett and Pinter, two writers of the avant-garde.[39] Since Albee does not explain what he means by these similarities, we can only guess that he is intimating some connection between the *themes* of Coward on the one hand and Beckett and Pinter on the other. Without explanation of some sort, such a statement can only be meaningless.

In this same introduction to the plays of Coward, Albee sets up three criteria for "all plays of any matter"—"literary excellence" [by which he means "rhythm and sound"], "dramatic sure-footedness," and "pertinence."[40] We find such criteria more than a little vague, notwithstanding his calling Coward "a dramatic mountain goat" with a better sense of *order* "from within" than of *form*. But, since Albee does mention "sound" a second time in this introduction (referring to the "precisely honed sense of form and sound" in the plays of Beckett and Pinter),[41] we may guess that "rhythm and sound"—a part of Coward's remarkable skill at writing dialogue—are among the chief qualities which appeal to Albee in Coward's plays. Of the collection generally, which includes Coward's *Blithe Spirit, Private Lives,* and *Hay Fever,* Albee says—whatever his reasons may be—"This book contains some very fine playwriting."[42]

Among other dramatists, besides those already mentioned in this section and earlier, Albee admits he might say some "harsh things" about Ibsen; but he likes Bertolt Brecht, when well performed, and Genet, Ionesco, Arrabal, and Ugo Betti.[43] This is by no means a complete list of Albee's favorite playwrights, but he briefly identifies himself with the "theater of the absurd" and speaks favorably of a few other modern writers such as Gogol and Büchner.[44]

VIII *Subjects and Methods*

A writer is known by the subjects he chooses and by how he handles them. "I'm not interested in the kind of problems that can be tied in a bundle at the third-act curtain," Albee tells us, defending his indeterminate ending of *Virginia Woolf*.[45] Like other avant-garde writers, he shows in his technique and method a remarkable disposition to make use of *any* means, the more metaphysical the better, to represent some of the grotesque effects characteristic of modern life. These range from "hellsappoppin" vaudeville to Frankensteinian horror; moreover, these may be coupled with highly serious or abjectly comic subjects to produce, when successful, a new, complicated kind of dramatic art.

William Flanagan has noted Albee's liking for "neo-burlesque comedy." "The cavortings of Bobby Clark or Bert Lahr reduced him to helpless laughter," he says. "The braying, henpecking female" of *The American Dream* Flanagan accordingly sees as "kith and kin to the Eternal Harridan that so relentlessly dogged the exacerbated footsteps of W. C. Fields, Groucho Marx, and James Thurber's Male Animal."[46] Since laughter and humor occupy so prominent a place in what the Existentialist writers regard as a proper response to their *Weltanschauung* of the absurdity of modern times, the resort to vaudevillean burlesque humor seems a reasonable direction for exploration by the "theater of the absurd." (Esslin distinguishes between the Existentialists and the Absurdists, but he has to grind rather finely for this distinction. The Existentialists, like Camus, popularized, after all, our concept of the *absurd*.)

IX *Music and Other Arts*

Albee's interest in music—whether symptomatic of his continuing bias for free experimentation in different literary forms, or indicative of a fixed, integral part of his general philosophy of art—certainly deserves more intensive study. "I always find a great association between plays and musical composition," he says; "composer friends of mine have told me that my work is related very strongly to musical form as they understand it."[47] With his fine ear for dialogue and with his "sense of movement in the theater," it is little wonder that to Albee "in a play, just as in a piece of music, there is a statement of theme, and variations, largo, allegro—the whole business."[48]

To William Flanagan, himself a composer, "an Albee play—once given its 'plot idea'—is conceived in structural blocks of cannily contrasted rhythmic and sonic textures. Consider the coda-like fragmentation of the two solo voices that bring *Who's Afraid of Virginia Woolf?* to its final unresolved cadence. Or consider the *agitato* solo aria . . . of 'The Zoo Story.' . . ."[49]

The fact remains, however, that *Bartleby,* the one major effort of Flanagan and Albee to collaborate on a distinctly musical production, failed dismally.[50] Actually, four different persons worked on this particular opera, which opened on January 24, 1961, and closed in early February. Herman Melville's short story, *Bartleby, the Scrivener,* generally acknowledged as a masterpiece of its kind, served Albee and James Hinton, Jr., as a starting point. They worked together adapting the story to the stage, while Flanagan wrote what has been described as a "vaguely atonal" score "full of difficult, craggy melodic content that Charles Ives invented." Although the adaptation from Melville was skillful enough, this work added up to "an indigestible one-act opera."[51] Harold Clurman kindly referred to it as an "honorable failure," placing the blame on the "inadequate two-piano version" of the musical score.[52]

We could make almost equally well, it seems to me, a case for Albee's sensitivity to the art of painting in such plays as *The Sandbox,* where the perspective of the scene on stage reminds one of a surrealistic canvas by De Chirico or Dali. Something of a connoisseur in painting, Albee's "perceptive criticism of work in graphic art" received favorable notice during his speaking engagement at Pratt Institute.[53]

X *Plays—How Long? And How Expensive?*

"I don't care whether a play is fifteen minutes or twelve hours long," writes Albee, "as long as it is satisfying and is written to its correct length."[54] To the query of how long a play should be, he has answered that each of his plays was "full-length because every play has its own duration."[55]

In his work as producer and director, as well as author, Albee invariably encounters the important problem of how much a play costs. Success in show business depends on an "angel's" willingness to risk money to pay at least the initial expenses of a play. The fact that Albee's early plays pivoted about small-sized casts probably represents an important element in the financial success of his undertakings. Economies of this kind tend to minimize the financial risk of the "angel."

Artistically, such economy may also contribute, if well-handled, to tightness of structure in plot and characterization. By using a minimum of props and spare sets—as in *The Sandbox, The American Dream, The Zoo Story,* and *The Death of Bessie Smith*—Albee has effected additional economy. In his Broadway productions, to be sure, he has given himself a much freer hand with respect to more conventional and more spectacular settings.

At least with respect to *Virginia Woolf,* his first Broadway production, Albee's insistence on his policy of "no out-of-town tryouts, no star-director arguments, no major doctoring of lines" paid financially and artistically.[56] The actors themselves were the "angels" of this production. Clinton Wilder, Richard Barr, and Albee secured Alan Schneider as director; and the stars—Uta Hagen, Arthur Hill, and George Grizzard—simply rented the Billy Rose Theater and started rehearsals. According to Lucas, "they brought in the show for a third of the usual cost."[57]

Albee's shorter plays, according to Stuart Little's account in the New York *Herald Tribune* of October 16, 1962, established amazing records for cheap but effective productions. Barr is quoted as saying that it cost twenty-five hundred dollars to "mount" *The Zoo Story,* thirty-five hundred dollars for *The American Dream,* and only two thousand dollars for *The Death of Bessie Smith.* He estimated the production cost of *Virginia Woolf* as about forty-five thousand dollars—still far less than the customary cost of producing a play on Broadway.

In the light of such facts and figures—but also not overlooking the part Albee's own theories and practices in dramatic art have contributed to the total picture—we can easily see one of the reasons for his sudden, phenomenal rise to a commanding position in the present-day American theater.

CHAPTER 3

Ancient Tragedy and Modern Absurdity

I *Classical Plot in Central Park*

*THE ZOO STORY** has a rather simple and easily comprehensible structure of three main parts that are climactically ordered. In the first part we are introduced to Jerry and Peter and to their differences with respect to person, background, economic status, marital status, literary taste, philosophy, desire for communication, the way they talk, and so on. The second part deals with the story of Jerry and the dog, and the third is the zoo story—what happened at the zoo.

The action of the entire drama is played against the background of *"foliage, trees, sky"* in Central Park in New York City on a summer Sunday afternoon in the present.[1] There are two park benches, and Peter is seated on one of them, reading a book, his habitual activity for such afternoons. The setting is definitely pinpointed as within visibility of the intersection of Fifth Avenue and Seventy-Fourth Street, on the east side of the park (12–13), within walking distance of Peter's residence between Lexington and Third Avenue on Seventy-Fourth Street (22).

The opposition between the characters of Jerry and Peter—the distinctive effect of part one—consists at least partly in the fact that Jerry lives on the west side of the park. The two men, however, do have one thing in common: they are nearly the same age. Peter, *"a man in his early forties,"* suggests *"a man younger"*; Jerry, in his later thirties, looks older, because of his *"fall from physical grace,"* hinted at by the fact that his *"lightly muscled body has begun to go to fat"* (11). Jerry also has *"a great weariness"* (11), possibly because of his long walk down to Washing-

---

*Used by permission of Coward-McCann, Inc., from THE ZOO STORY, THE SANDBOX and THE DEATH OF BESSIE SMITH by Edward Albee; © 1960.

ton Square and back again, which he tells about, but possibly, too, because of the totality of his life-experience—one so different in kind from that of the favored Peter.

The contrast between the two characters, as already indicated, is revealed by the progress of the topics they discuss. The conversation actually begins with Jerry's forcing himself upon Peter's attention by announcing three times, progressively louder, that he has been to the zoo. After Jerry discovers where he is—he had lost his way during his long hike—he moves the talk along by a series of intrusive questions, or they appear so to Peter, who wants to be let alone. But Jerry persists; for, as he explains, he had felt, for at least once, a deep desire to communicate with another human being instead of mouthing such usual remarks as "give me a beer, or where's the john, or what time does the feature go on, or keep your hands to yourself, buddy . . ." (19). "Every once in a while," he says, "I like to talk to somebody, really *talk;* like to get to know somebody, know all about him" (19).

This isolation, a common element of life in large cities, Jerry feels challenged to combat—vigorously, aggressively, and, as it happens, to the death. Thus the theme of the play bears directly on a current social problem and at the same time on the deeply philosophical subjects handled by Ionesco, Beckett, and Genet—the breakdown of language, the attempt to live by illusion, the alienation of the individual from his fellow men, the terrible loneliness of every living human being.

Jerry's questions to Peter elicit such facts about the latter's life as that he thinks he can avoid cancer by smoking a pipe, that he is acquainted with the life of Freud, that he is educated, that he reads *Time* magazine, that he owns two television sets (an extra one for his two daughters), that he wanted a son but that his wife would have no more children, that he doesn't really want cats but that his daughters and wife have brought both cats and parakeets into his household, that he has "an executive position with . . . a small publishing house" handling textbooks, and makes "around eighteen thousand a year" (21), that, though he prides himself on his good taste in literature, he cannot tell Jerry the difference between two such different writers as Baudelaire and J. P. Marquand (24), that he is disappointed to find out that Jerry doesn't live in Greenwich Village, and that he is reticent generally (22) and embarrassed about discussing his sex life (32).

In the course of his cross-examination of Peter, Jerry shows no reluctance whatever about revealing his own private life. The following points come out about him: he is not married, but apparently has had plenty of one-night sex experiences with women and was even, at one stage in his development, a homosexual. He resents Peter's patronizing attitude toward him; he has had an entirely different kind of education—the "school of hard knocks." He is aware of the finicky economic class distinctions that seem to mean so much to some Americans, such distinctions as the difference between the "upper-middle-middle-class" and the "lower-upper-middle class." And he is direct and honest.

He lives on the West Side under circumstances far different from Peter's, in a "laughably small room" on the top floor, between Columbus Avenue and Central Park West. He is observant of his neighbors—the Puerto Rican family that entertains a lot; the woman who cries determinedly all day; the homosexual who plucks his eyebrows "with Buddhist concentration" (26) but who keeps his hands to himself; and the fat, elderly, gin-soaked landlady of whose sweaty lust he (Jerry) is the object (33). He seems strangely affected by the fact that he has never seen and will never get to know a person who lives in a room within a few feet of his own: "And in the other front room, there's somebody living there, but I don't know who it is. I've never seen who it is. Never. Never ever" (26).

In contrast to Peter's "apartment in the East Seventies" and his "one wife, two daughters, two cats and two parakeets," and other possessions, Jerry's personal accessories include such items as can openers, a hot plate, a few clothes, a knife, a fork, "eight or nine books," a "pack of pornographic playing cards," some rocks which he has picked up on the beach, love letters, and, among other things, two empty picture frames (27). Asked about these, he explains the sordid details of his mother's adulterous tour of the Southern states, ending with her death in Alabama, and, shortly afterward, his drunken father's accidentally stepping in front of "a somewhat moving city omnibus" (28). Following this "vaudeville act" (28) had come what he calls "a terribly middle-European joke," the death of his mother's sister "on the afternoon of my high school graduation" (29). (Jerry characterizes her as having done "all things dourly: sleeping, eating, working, praying." [28–29]). Apparently she had reared him from the time he was ten and a half—after his parents' departure. Despite these "hard knocks," Jerry does not feel sorry for himself; he is tough-minded about all aspects of his personal experience.

But Jerry suffers from certain unanswered questions arising from his experience, and these questions the other two parts of the play dramatize for us. At the beginning of part two, "The Story of Jerry and the Dog," Jerry prefaces his remarks by saying: "What I am going to tell you has something to do with how sometimes it's necessary to go a long distance out of the way in order to come back a short distance correctly" (36). The rather profound answer to this enigmatic opening becomes clear only at the end of this story, although the audience already knows at the merely physical level that Jerry has trudged all the way down to Washington Square and back again. Too, the audience is ready for the story because Jerry, in his account of his landlady's sweaty lust and his way of putting her off—by referring to their love of the previous day, "and the day before," so that she actually "believes and relives what never happened"—also has mentioned to Peter that the landlady's companion in these encounters is a "black monster of a dog" (34). This animal forthwith becomes Jerry's antagonist in part two of the play.

Albee presents the animal vividly. The dog is old, misused, and black all over except for its bloodshot eyes and the red, open sore on its right front paw. The dog "almost always has an erection . . . of sorts. [And] "that's red, too." But "when he bares his fangs," "there's a gray-yellow-white color" (36). From the first, the dog had unmistakably declared his intention of biting him, as Jerry explains: "I worried about that animal the very first minute I met him. Now, animals don't take to me like Saint Francis had birds hanging off him all the time. What I mean is: animals are indifferent to me . . . like people (*He smiles slightly*) . . . most of the time. But this dog wasn't indifferent. From the very beginning he'd snarl and then go for me, to get one of my legs" (36–37).

Thurber has a somewhat similar dog in his well-known story *The Dog That Bit People*, but his animal bit indiscriminately and ubiquitously. The curious thing about Albee's dog is that he apparently does not bother the other roomers—only Jerry—and only when Jerry comes in, never when he goes out. After over a week of narrow escapes and torn trousers, Jerry decides to "kill the dog with kindness" and, if that doesn't work, to "just kill him" (37).

To his great surprise, neither plan succeeds. First, when he offers the dog "six perfectly good hamburgers with not enough pork in them to make it disgusting," the dog eats them ravenously, "making sounds in his throat like a woman," then tries to eat the paper bag they came in, and finally, after a quiescent moment in which Jerry thinks the dog smiles at him, "BAM" (38), it snarls and charges him again. Second, when he poisons the dog, it becomes deathly ill—so ill, in fact, that the drunken landlady sobers up and asks Jerry to pray for her "puppykins." But both "puppykins" and landlady recover: the former, its health; the latter, her thirst.

After this episode Jerry and the dog have a confrontation—Jerry now "unafraid" and the "beast" looking "better for his scrape with the nevermind" (41). They stare at each other for a long time; and, "during that twenty seconds or two hours that" they look into each other's eyes, they *make contact* (41). Jerry, who now refers to the dog as his *friend*, says: "I loved the dog now, and I wanted him to love me. I had tried to love, and I had tried to kill, and both had been unsuccessful by themselves . . . I hoped that the dog would understand . . . it's just that if you can't deal with people, you have to make a start somewhere. WITH ANIMALS! . . . with . . . some day, with people" (42–43).

This passage brings us close to the theme, as does the one that immediately follows it. The contact made during that moment, it seems, had been only a transient one; for now, as Jerry says, whenever they meet they both regard each other "with a mixture of sadness and suspicion, and then we feign *indifference*" [(43) (my italics)]. An "understanding" has been reached: the dog no longer rushes him; he no longer feeds or poisons the dog.

> I have gained solitary free passage, if that much further loss can be said to be gain. I have learned that neither kindness nor cruelty by themselves, independent of each other, creates any effect beyond themselves; and I have learned that the two combined, together, at the same time, are the *teaching emotion* [my italics]. And what is gained is loss. And what has been the result: the dog and I have attained a compromise; more of a bargain really. We neither love nor hurt because we do not try to reach each other. And, *was* trying to feed the dog an act of love? And, per-

> haps, was the dog's attempt to bite me *not* an act of love? If we can so misunderstand, well then, why have we invented the word love in the first place? (43–44)

Following this important passage of what Aristotle would call *Thought* (see *Poetics*), Albee has indicated silence for emphasis and has also written into the stage directions that at this point Jerry moves to Peter's bench and sits down beside him for the first time in the play. At the same time the playwright makes Jerry announce, "The Story of Jerry and the Dog: the end," thus unmistakably bringing to an effective and highly dramatic close this important second part of the play.

Although the transition to part three may seem somewhat long, it is nevertheless effective in doing two rather necessary things. First, it brings Jerry and Peter into an intensity of conflict that their differences of background and character had only begun to develop in part one. Second, it provides the motive for Peter's remaining on the scene in spite of this difference in character. An intense and fierce struggle between Jerry and Peter is necessary, for it is ultimately the cause of what happens at the final climactic point of the play—the death of Jerry at Peter's hands. If one character is going to kill another at the end of the play, the author must obviously provide preparation for such an act.

Albee's procedure in handling this preparation shows remarkable skill. He begins by having Jerry ask Peter about selling the story concerning the dog to the *Reader's Digest* in order to "make a couple of hundred bucks for *The Most Unforgettable Character I've Ever Met.*" This fair question is put to Peter since he knows all about how to make money in publishing, but it also points up the great difference between Jerry and Peter. For Peter, Jerry suggests, the only value of the story might be its potential as lucre; for Jerry, however, what happened between him and the dog represents possibly the most exciting and meaningful experience of his entire life—something that has nothing at all to do with money value. So, when Peter says he does not understand why a perfect stranger should spill out his private life to him in such a tale, Jerry remonstrates with a furious whisper, "That's a lie." For he knows that Peter is not only educated (at least superficially) but is also experienced and intelligent enough to understand exactly what he (Jerry) is trying to express. Whatever this is, it has to do with the common humanity between the two men, or between any two men; and since Peter refuses to acknowledge it, it must be acted out and dramatized in a way he will never forget—which is exactly what happens in part three.

Peter's refusal to "understand" and his not wanting to hear any more about Jerry, the landlady, or the dog (45) depress Jerry and solidify the superficial but extreme opposition between the characters. Jerry says at this point, ". . . of course you don't understand. (*In a monotone, wearily*) I don't live in your block; I'm not married to two parakeets, or whatever your setup is. I am a permanent transient, and my home is the sickening roominghouses on the West Side of New York City, which is the greatest city in the world. Amen" (45).

After a little desultory conversation (46), Peter looks at his watch and threatens to leave. To prevent his departure, Jerry tickles him into helplessness, into willingness to listen to the second story—what happened at the zoo. Here Peter begins the process of self-discovery, for he notes with surprise that he cannot quite explain what had happened to him, what had caused him to succumb to the almost hysterical fit of laughing. Even Jerry remarks, "Yes, that was very funny, Peter. I wouldn't have expected it" (49).

After this five-page transition—or interruption of the action—Jerry continues as follows:

> Now I'll let you in on what happened at the zoo; but first, I should tell you why I went to the zoo. I went to the zoo to find out more about the way people exist with animals, and the way animals exist with each other, and with people too. It probably wasn't a fair test, what with everyone separated by bars from everyone else, the animals for the most part from each other, and always the people from the animals. But if it's a zoo, that's the way it is. (*He pokes* PETER *on the arm*) Move over. (49)

This speech markes the beginning not only of part three but also of a series of moves on Jerry's part to unseat Peter from his bench. At first Peter responds with friendliness and gives him more room; but, as Jerry's requests become progressively less polite and always rougher and more demanding, unreasonably demanding, until he at last wants the whole bench—"my bench," as he calls it—Peter is aroused to fighting fury. Almost in tears, he shouts, "GET AWAY FROM MY BENCH!"

Jerry replies tauntingly, "Why? You have everything in the world you want; you've told me about your home, and your family, and *your own* little zoo. You have everything, and now you want this bench. Are these the things men fight for? Tell me, Peter, is this bench, this iron and this wood, is this your honor? Is this the thing in the world you'd fight for? Can you think of anything more absurd?" (55–56)

Peter refuses to discuss the question of honor with Jerry, who, he says, wouldn't understand it anyway. Jerry continues adding insult to injury: "This is probably the first time in your life you've had anthing more trying to face than changing your cat's toilet box. Stupid! Don't you have any idea, not even the slightest, what other people *need*?" (56). When Peter replies that Jerry doesn't *need* this particular bench, Jerry shoots back, "Yes; yes, I do." Peter, "*quivering*" with anger, lets out that he has come there for years, has had "hours of pleasure, great satisfaction, right here . . . This is my bench, and you have no right to take it away from me" (56). And Jerry retorts: "Fight for it, then. Defend yourself; defend your bench." He also insults him further by calling him "a vegetable," a "slightly nearsighted one . . ."(57).

At this crisis the two men are ready for battle. Jerry clicks open a wicked-looking toad-stabber. The Westside jungle has at least conditioned him for this eventuality, and he rises to it "*lazily*," but nonetheless confidently and fully equipped, quietly ready for combat. Peter, on the other hand, awakes to the reality of the situation with horror and melodramatically cries out, "You are mad! You're stark raving mad! YOU'RE GOING TO KILL ME!" (58). Jerry tosses the knife at Peter's feet, saying "You have the knife and we'll be more evenly matched" (58).

When Peter refuses to accept this challenge, Jerry in turn grows infuriated. He rushes Peter, grabs him by the collar, and says with great intensity, "Now you pick up that knife and you fight me. You fight for your self-respect; you fight for that goddamned bench" (58). But, when Peter only struggles to escape, Jerry begins slapping him in the face. He slaps him each time he says *fight* during the following speech: ". . . fight, you miserable bastard; fight for that bench; fight for your parakeets; fight for your cats, fight for your two daughters; fight for your wife; fight for your manhood, you pathetic little vegetable" (59). Finally, he spits in Peter's face and insults him still again by saying, "You couldn't even get your wife with a male child" (59).

All this is at last too much for Peter. He picks up the knife and backs off a little, breathing heavily. He holds the knife far out in front of him rigidly, frozen into defensiveness; then Jerry, realizing they have reached a point of no return, sighs heavily and with a "So be it!" "*charges* PETER *and impales himself on the knife*" (59).

From this point to the end of the play, Jerry dies. But, before the last breath of life has escaped him, he clarifies the theme of the play in two fairly long speeches. In the second, the less important, he congratulates Peter on the defense of his honor, although at the loss of his bench; for Peter, he says, will never return to it because of what has happened. He also says Peter is not really a *vegetable* but an *animal*. In the first, or more important of the two speeches, he thanks Peter. (Peter is aghast at this gratitude, for he knows he has been the means of Jerry's death—the agent and unwitting executioner, despite Jerry's suicidal act.) "Oh, Peter," he says, "I was so afraid I'd drive you away ... You don't know how afraid I was you'd go away and leave me" (60). Then he goes on to say,

> And now I'll tell you what happened at the zoo. I think ... I think this is what happened at the zoo ... I think, I think that while I was at the zoo I decided that I would walk north ... *northerly rather* ... until I found you ... or somebody ... and I decided that I would talk to you ... I would tell you things ... and things that I would tell you would ... Well, here we are. You see? Here we *are*. ... And now I've told you what you wanted to know, haven't I? And now you know all about what happened at the zoo. And now you know what you'll see in your TV, and the face I told you about ... you remember ... the face I told you about ... my face, the face you see right now. (60–61) [First italics are mine.][2]

What happened at the zoo, according to Jerry, had simply been the decision to walk in a northward direction and to try to find some person with whom he could make contact. For he had not really made contact with the dog (in the second part of the play), it will be recalled, although they had come to "an understanding" (43). Jerry expresses this situation this way: "We neither love nor hurt because we do not try to reach each other" (44). Yet Jerry says that, from his experience with the dog, he had learned "the teaching emotion," that combination of kindness and cruelty that formulates, for him at least, life itself (44).

This same formula, this "teaching emotion," plays itself out in the grim ending. When Jerry pierces the defensive armor of Peter, he *makes contact* with him in a way he never had with the dog.[3] And he takes comfort in his success, even though it is achieved at the expense of his life—with cruelty, *fated*, as it were, in the chain of events. For he says: "I came unto you (*He laughs, so faintly*) and you have comforted me. Dear Peter" (61). And he asks: ". . . could I have planned all this? No . . . no, I couldn't have. But I think I did" (60).

II *Problems and Comments*

There are three separate problems in this episode, as I see it, that Albee thrusts deliberately into the attention of the reader or the playgoer. First, there is the problem of the biblical language and what he means to convey by his use of it; second, there is the face on the television screen, alluded to earlier (16, 19); third, certain implications concerning human existence, either particularized or generalized. For it seems to me that Albee is working partly, but only partly, from an Existentialist position.

Earlier in the story of his encounter with the Dog, Jerry had also paraphrased the Bible, *with irony*, saying, "AND IT CAME TO PASS THAT THE BEAST WAS DEATHLY ILL," just after he had fed it the poisoned hamburgers.[4] Two sentences after this quotation he tells of his landlady's maudlin announcement that "God had struck her puppy-dog a surely fatal blow" and her request that he "pray" for its recovery (44). Thus the audience is prepared for the kind of diction we discover at the end of the play.

But what does Albee intend? Or perhaps, more accurately, what do the words suggest? In the New Testament, Peter betrays Christ instead of comforting him.[5] In the play, Peter's comfort of Jerry amounts to his not leaving him. But Jerry's faint laughter (61), as he states his gratitude, shows his insight; for he knows that such comfort as he has managed to draw out of Peter has not been freely given; it has been supplied not only with indifference and reluctance but perhaps also with latent *cruelty* (the other part of the "teaching emotion")—the cold steel of the knife that had brought him death. Therefore, the passage can only be construed as *ironical,* as in the earlier biblical paraphrase.

As for the face on the television screen, Jerry's mention of it early in the play, when he first encounters Peter (16), seems at first glance to be part of his tough-minded attitude toward himself. It is as if he were arguing, against his better judgment, the importance of his private visit to the zoo by placing it in the same category with more public and possibly more newsworthy events—such as appear daily in metropolitan newspapers and on nation-wide television broadcasts. Such an argument shows Jerry's strong individualism and makes him an appealing character, particularly as it is voiced in rebellion against the strong pressures that beset struggling individualists of all kinds in big cities like New York. Albee emphasizes the point by making Peter ask, shortly afterward (19), "What were you saying about the zoo . . . that I'd read about it, or see . . . ?" Jerry, however, puts him off by saying he will tell him about it soon. At this point in the play, all Jerry wants is conversation—a listener at any price.

At the end of the play, however, where Jerry says, "And now you know what you'll see in your TV, and the face I told you about . . . my face . . . ," the earlier prophecy, or preparation, has been fulfilled. Murder, suicide, and accidental death belong to the category of the sensational that makes up so large a part of newspaper and television news; Jerry's death (what Aristotle and the Greeks called "tragic incident" in a tragedy) combines all three—murder, suicide, and accident. How, then, can we explain Jerry's elaborate precautions to see that Peter will not be detected as participant in this event? (He wipes Peter's fingerprints off the knife, reminds him to take his book along with him, and urges him to hurry away. [62]) The answer must surely lie in what Jerry knows about Peter: the kind of person he has discovered him to be. Whatever else he is, Peter is bookish; introspective; and, above all, highly conformist—in short, the kind of person who can never forget this incident, or Jerry. The face, then, that he will see on the television screen will be one that he projects there himself, the face of Jerry, one that will forever come between him and the other sensational events that we so often see on this medium.

Finally, the play exhibits certain characteristics of Existentialism. It impresses us, especially that part of it dealing with Jerry's life, as a struggle for existence—in the jungle of the city. The conflict of values, the attack on the bourgeois code that Jerry continues as long as there is breath in him, is acted out on a park bench and is surely one of the basic situations of human existence that Sartre talks of as constituting dramatizable material.[6] Moreover, Jerry qualifies as an Existentialist hero: he makes his choices freely. His decision to impale himself on the knife Peter is stiffly holding is a deliberate act. "So be it," he says simply; but he nonetheless knows full well exactly what he is doing.[7]

Jerry also represents what another writer refers to as "the strange, inaccessible self [that] . . . remains when a person has lost the whole world but not himself, the very real inner impassioned feel of self, the self beyond the transcendental unity" of Kant which is "unknowable and incommunicable."[8] His death is a deliberate act of protest against the wrongs of the city, the injustice of the system, the bourgeois values that cause *nausea,* the feeling of life being lived in a void, the isolation of man. The play suggests that the price of survival under these conditions may be the murder of our fellow man, even when accomplished accidentally or unwittingly. We have heard this cliché of men's expendability bandied about by militarists in connection with the rationalizing of dropping atomic bombs to end war, but not much with respect to the cannibalism of our socioeconomic system. As Albee presents this human condition, it becomes completely absurd; and he makes this point strongly when at the end he lets Jerry taunt Peter, the survivor, with this little grotesquerie: "Hurry away, your parakeets are making the dinner . . . the cats . . . are setting the table . . ." (62).

That man's condition is not only absurd but also subhuman is perhaps what, in the last analysis, Albee means by the title, *The Zoo Story.* Yet for Jerry, who knows life closely and well, all men are divided into two classes—vegetable and animal; the former comprise those who merely subsist and the latter those who are willing to fight and kill, as animals do, for survival. At first he is unwilling to grant Peter the high praise of admission to the animal class, but ultimately, when dying, he does: "And Peter, I'll tell you something now; you're not really a vegetable . . .

you're an animal." But it is significant that no terms—other than vegetable and animal—are used to describe the condition of man.

Jerry is in the midst of a rebellion against this condition, and wants desperately to "make a start somewhere," with animals if not with people; with anything, as he says eloquently in his account of his earlier experience with the dog; or even with a "GOD WHO IS A COLORED QUEEN WHO WEARS A KIMONO AND PLUCKS HIS EYEBROWS, WHO IS A WOMAN WHO CRIES WITH DETERMINATION BEHIND HER CLOSED DOOR . . . with God who, I'm told, turned his back on the whole thing some time ago . . . in this humiliating excuse for a jail . . ." (42–43). To orthodox believers, this statement will seem blasphemous. But let us not forget that even the orthodox Christian divinity once took human form.

And let us remember, too, that the Existentialist view of life as a trap is really not so very different from the older Puritan concept of the world as a vale of tears with a possibly more restricted liberty of choice, or freedom of the will, than the Existentialists offer us. If, then, we reject the view of God presented in *The Zoo Story*, one to which Jerry is driven in desperation, we should not necessarily conclude that Albee speaks from an atheist, rather than a theist, position. For the stage directions that Albee has written for the last speech of the play, "Oh . . . my . . . God"—in which, with full consistency of character, Jerry continues his derision of Peter right to the end—call for the delivery of these words in a "*combination of scornful mimicry and supplication*" (62).

We also must always remember that, simply because Albee treats Jerry this way in a work of fiction, we cannot really make any very valid conclusions about Albee's own personal religious convictions, which may be entirely different from those of any character in his play. In summary, we must conclude either that the character of Jerry is slightly inconsistent here, because of his earlier representations of an ineffectual or indifferent deity (42–43), or that the peculiar brand of Existentialism offered is nearer to orthodoxy or to the theism of Marcel than to the atheism of Sartre or Camus.[9] It does not necessarily follow, of course, that, because Jerry feels that God is indifferent to human suffering, he is bound to assume that God does not exist. However Albee might defend the consistency of his characterization of Jerry by arguing the indifference or the nonexistence of God and the influence of either on Jerry's final statement, the fact remains that the tragic effect is heightened by Albee's inclusion of the word *supplication,* difficult as it is for any actor to express the complex tonal combination of simultaneous mimicry and prayer for which the author calls (62).

III *Tragedy in the Greek Manner*

The Zoo Story stands up well as a tragedy in the Greek manner: its plot hangs together well in terms of its cause-effect sequence of episodes or main parts, and it contains a reversal and more than one discovery. If, in considering the *reversal,* we conceive the plot in terms of Jerry's struggle for existence against forces that threaten his highly individualistic, nonconformist character, as well as his protest against the consequent isolation that a conformist society punishes him with for daring to assert such individualism, then his confrontation with Peter, a representative of that society, becomes a kind of crisis or a climax to his entire life. And when Jerry discovers that he can pierce the barrier of this ever increasing isolation—and at the same time maintain his integrity—only at the cost of his life, and when he consequently rushes on the knife held by Peter, the plot reverses itself.

Until this moment in the plot there has never been any doubt about the ability of Jerry (the nonconformist, the poisoner of the dog, the confident battler willing to even the odds by letting Peter have the knife) to *survive.* On the contrary, he has always given the impression of being able to take care of himself. He has been bothered, deeply bothered, to be sure, by certain problems—his landlady's repulsive love-making, his unhappy neighbors, his episode with the mean dog, his sense of growing alienation—but there has never been any real doubt about survival as such. He has always been able to outrun the dog, to keep homosexuals at bay.

But now there is real doubt; his former good fortune turns to bad fortune. Peter picks up the knife, goaded by Jerry's insults. When Peter takes his stand, no alternative exists for Jerry. Given this situation—the aroused emotions of the combatants, the depth of their conflict, Jerry's past—there is absolutely no other way for him to make contact with the conditioned, calloused Peter (who,

I repeat, represents the coldly adamantine exterior which society turns on the nonconformist) than by lunging at the knife. Jerry consequently triumphs over Peter and shows the superiority of his code and his character. He becomes in his death a kind of hero, and the playgoer experiences a genuine catharsis of pity and fear.[10]

Turning now to *discovery* or *recognition*, we immediately observe that we have a double one.[11] We have already considered Jerry's discovery or recognition that there is no other course open for him except suicide. We have seen how Peter becomes, at least momentarily for him, an enemy. And this change from friendliness to hate on Jerry's part is what Aristotle means by *recognition* —"a change from ignorance to knowledge, producing love or hate between the persons destined by the poet for good or bad fortune."[12] For Peter, too, there is a *recognition*, beginning at the point where he thinks Jerry is going to kill him (58). But by a skillful twist Albee surprises the audience (and this is the proper effect the reversal of the plot should have, as long as it follows the law of probability) and makes Peter actually kill Jerry. With the realization of what he has done, Peter changes from his earlier tolerance for Jerry to horror of what Jerry has made him—a murderer. *Horror* is perhaps not the same as Aristotle's "hate," but Albee does speak of love and hate together as the teaching emotion; and such a mixture of love and hate is the emotional state of both protagonist and antagonist as the drama closes. At first, Peter weeps, repeating again and again "Oh my God, oh my God." Then, at Jerry's injunction, he begins to "*stagger away*," and the last we hear from him is a pitiful offstage howl, "OH MY GOD!" (61–62). Thus the absurdity of survival in the twentieth century is dramatized with peculiarly Grecian effectiveness.

CHAPTER 4

Pity and Fear in Miniature

I *The Text Analyzed*

THE SANDBOX is the shortest of Albee's one-act plays, requiring only fourteen minutes' time in the theater (5). A memorial to his own grandmother (139), the play deals with the death of an old lady. Grandma is eighty-six years old; and her daughter and son-in-law, aged fifty-five and sixty, respectively, are waiting for her to die (143). Outside this triangular family situation there are two other characters, the Young Man and the Musician. The Young Man, age twenty-five, is described as "*good-looking, well-built*" and as dressed "*in a bathing suit*" (143). With his beating and fluttering calisthenics he typifies the Angel of Death (144), although this fact is not known to the other characters. The Musician, according to Albee, should be of "*no particular age, but young would be nice*" (143).

The curtain goes up on a scene at the beach—sand, water, and sky, in that order, are in the background. In the foreground, far stage-right, "*two simple chairs set side by side*" face the audience (143–44). Far stage-left shows a single chair and a music stand for the Musician, who faces stage-right when seated. Between these two, at stage center and to the back, there stands a slightly elevated large sandbox, such as children play in, with a toy pail and a shovel (144).

Although the play covers a little more than twenty-four hours—starting with "*brightest day*" and progressing to "*deepest night*" and the birth of a new day (144)—the action, or plot, falls into six divisions or scenes. In the first of these Mommy and Daddy appear on the beach, and Daddy complains that it is cold. Mommy accuses him of being silly, for it is actually as warm as toast, she says as she waves flirtatiously to the Young Man in the bathing suit. "Look at that nice young man over there: *he* doesn't think it's cold," she says, and speaks to him (144). The Young Man smiles endearingly at her and calls "Hi!" (145). After this exchange Mommy, who is described as "*imposing*" and well-dressed (145), persuades Daddy to help her in disposing of Grandma. Daddy, a thin, little gray man, has to do whatever Mommy says. When Mommy tells the Musician he can come on stage, he then enters, puts his music on the stand, and prepares to play; but he does not play until she rather highhandedly tells him to do so.

In the second scene Mommy and Daddy drag in Grandma, carrying her under the armpits. She holds her tiny figure rigid; her knees are drawn up; and an expression of bewilderment and fear is on her face. When they dump her into the sandbox, she cries like a baby, throws sand at Mommy, and screams at Daddy. Mommy continues flirting with the young man in the bathing suit, who steadily flashes his endearing smile; and she also maintains her "bossing" of Daddy and the Musician. In response to Daddy's question as to what they do now, after having deposited Grandma in the sandbox, Mommy replies, "We . . . wait. We . . . sit here . . . and wait . . . that's what we do" (148).

After more music, which apparently serves as a transition between these earlier scenes (149), Grandma, in the third scene, begins talking to the Young Man; complaining about her bad treatment from her daughter, who had married for money; and telling about her own past life. At an early age she had married a farmer, who had died when she was but thirty years old, leaving her alone to raise her unpleasant daughter. When she asks the Young Man where he is from, he replies, Southern California. When she asks him what his name is, he says, "They haven't given me one yet" (151). On his mentioning the word "studio," she suggests that he may be an actor. He says, "Yes, I am." Finally, she looks up at the sky and shouts off stage, "Shouldn't it be getting dark now, dear?" (152). The rather obvious air of improvisation throughout this play reminds one of Pirandello's *Six Characters in Search of an Author,* or *Tonight We Improvise,* or Thornton Wilder's *Our Town.*

In scene four it is "*deepest night,*" and spotlights are focused on each player (152). The Musician plays through nearly the entire scene although, at Grandma's suggestion, he keeps the music "nice and soft" (153). Four successively louder off-stage rumbles convey, tonally, a closer approach to Grandma's death. The fourth rumble is characterized in Albee's stage direction as "*violent,*" and at the same moment all the lights go out except that on the face of the Young Man (154). When Mommy begins to weep during this scene, Daddy urges her to be brave; but Grandma mocks, "That's right, kid; be brave. You'll bear up; you'll get over it" (154). After the fourth loud rumble, near the end of the scene, the Musician stops playing, Mommy gasps out two long "Oh's," and an ominous silence ensues, after which Grandma's last speech in the scene reads, "Don't put the lights up yet . . . I'm not ready; I'm not quite ready. (*Silence*) All right dear . . . I'm about done" (154).

When the lights come on again in scene five, it is a new day; and we see Grandma, lying propped on an elbow and with her body half covered with sand, "*busily*" shoveling more sand over herself with her free hand (155). Thinking, wishfully, that Grandma is finally buried, Mommy brightens into what we might at first suspect as a post-funeral mood: "We must put away our tears, take off our mourning . . . and face the future. It's our duty" (155). But Grandma is not yet dead, and she again mimicks Mommy, whose sorrow is evidently not so profound as to interfere with her again waving at the handsome Young Man (still in the bathing suit), who again smiles his endearing smile at her. Then, with hands crossed upon her breast and holding the toy shovel, Grandma pretends she is dead, as Mommy delivers herself of certain admiring ejaculations about the lovely appearance of what she believes to be the corpse of her mother. At the end of this scene, during which the Musician again plays continuously, Mommy tells him he can stop now (supposedly because she thinks her mother dead) and stay around or go for a swim if he likes. She and Daddy both congratulate each other on their bravery.

In the sixth and last scene, however, Grandma does meet death. Still alive, she discovers that she can no longer move. The Young Man, who up to this time has been flexing his muscles like any handsome gymnast on a beach, now amateurishly announces himself to her as the Angel of Death. And with this, Grandma's second discovery, he kisses her. To her surprise, she finds the kiss of this polite, modest, half-apologetic young man "very nice," very pleasant (157). She closes her eyes and smiles sweetly. She compliments him, saying "you did that very well, dear . . . you've got a quality" (158). After he smiles and respectfully thanks her very much and after she very politely says "You're welcome . . . dear," he puts his hands on top of hers; and she dies (158). The Musician continues to play as the curtain slowly descends on the tableau, his music having been instigated at the start of this scene by a nod from the powerful Young Man.

Although the play includes six quite separate scenes, we can easily see (now that we have examined it as a whole) that it also has a fairly clear beginning-middle-end logic. Scene one, for example, not only introduces the characters but also presents Mommy's scheme to dispose of Grandma. Scenes two through five show the failure of this plan. Scene six reveals an unexpected turn of events and brings the play to a satisfying close.

II *The Characters in Conflict*

The five characters in the play have obviously been selected with great care and in accord with the artistic principle of economy of means. Grandma, for example, is not only the leading character, or *protagonist*, but also the *chorus*. Her mimicking of Mommy and her mocking of Daddy, as well as her early cries, some of which are like screams of antagonism or growls of disgust, reinforce the self-revealing speeches of these two unsympathetic characters, just as the chanted explanations of the Greek chorus in ancient tragedies underlined similar aspects of the characterization and the action. In one or two places Grandma also functions as the stage manager or director, for she calls out directions to the stage hand about dimming the lights and she tells the musician how to play his music—"Keep it nice and soft"—in the night scene signifying the approach of death (153).

Study of the conflicting forces in *The Sandbox* shows us how central the character of Grandma is. On the surface, it appears that we have two pairs of characters struggling against each other—Mommy and Daddy in the antagonist group (who are really trying to bury Grandma, as we see by their symbolic action of heartlessly dumping her into the sandbox); and Grandma and the Young Man in the protagonist group. This ostensible pairing of unsympathetic and sympathetic characters overshadows a less obvious conflict—that between Grandma, an admirable old lady full of spiritual vitality, and the Young Man, the Angel of Death. Despite the Young Man's modesty and politeness, he is, after all, the Angel of Death; and, while Grandma recognizes that her life cannot go on forever (154), she nevertheless still has a certain spark of spunky rebelliousness and fight left in her—enough, as a matter of fact, so that the manner of her final encounter with death becomes a suspenseful question: Will she fight to the end? Or will she resign herself to the inevitable—the superior power of the Angel of Death?

Grandma struggles against the injustice of her daughter's and her son-in-law's treatment of her more than she does against the Young Man, whom she finds attractive, pleasant, sympathetic. Although his approach is gradual, he, when the time comes, accomplishes his work quickly and efficiently—even apologetically, so polite is he—with a kiss and a laying on of hands that resembles a benediction. This kind of treatment Grandma will accept. But in resentment of her daughter's and son-in-law's standing around and not only waiting for her to die but even hastening the process, she throws sand and yells at them menacingly.

In the course of the action, Grandma moves from "*puzzlement and fear*" to acceptance (146). When she says "You're welcome . . . dear" to the Angel of Death at the end of the play (158), we see her conquer her fear of the unknown and admire her all the more. We begin to sense her heroic nature, for it is death and dying she struggles against, sympathetic as the Young Man, to her surprise, and relief, finally turns out to be after her discovery of his essential nature.

Grandma is just as sensitive to the Young Man's physical power and beauty as Mommy—in fact, more so. When he flexes his muscles for her and asks, "Isn't that something?," she answers, "Boy, oh boy; I'll say. Pretty good" (150). Her conversation with and admiration of the Young Man is interspersed with the story of her life and hard times, which arouses sympathy for her, particularly as she stresses the fact that she is neither complaining nor feeling sorry for herself.

III *Pity and Fear: Arousal and Purgation*

Grandma effectively arouses pity and fear in the audience. We *pity* her because she deserves better than she has received.

After the early death of her husband, after a hard life spent in sacrificing to her undeserving daughter, after being uprooted from her natural setting on the farm (her husband having been a farmer) and transported to the city, where she was treated like a dog, she deserves something more than merely dying. But it would be unrealistic for her not to die, for the expectation of her dying has been established from almost the beginning of this play when she is carried in and dumped in the sandbox.

We *fear* for Grandma because in Aristotelian terms she is a person like ourselves—neither entirely good nor bad. In addition, her fragility, because of her great age as well as because of the great powers arrayed against her—Mommy with her "imposing" vigor, Daddy with his wealth, the Young Man with his immense power as the Angel of Death (144, 157)—makes us sense that her position is indeed precarious. The four off-stage rumbles (153–54) especially arouse in the audience a feeling of the Young Man's power; and, since we tend to identify ourselves with Grandma, fear is aroused in us. The arousal of this fear continues until the point where the Young Man kisses her; then we are fearful that he may severely hurt her. After all, there are various ways of suffering in the death of the body.

Purgation of fear and pity in *The Sandbox* results from the demonstration that Grandma is not going to suffer more—from our comprehension that death, contrary to our usual expectations, is, for her, a sweet, welcome experience. If pity and fear are not only effectively aroused but also competently purged in this play, if these are the distinctive and characteristic emotions making up the effect of the play, we must conclude that the play is a *tragedy*. And so it is—a serious tragedy—well flavored with irony and absurdity—from Grandma's juvenile antics in the sandbox and her reference to her daughter as a "big cow" to the awkward embarrassment of the Young Man. Touches like these may not exhale the high seriousness of tone that critics like Krutch might like to find in modern tragedy, but we must remember that we are living in the age of the "absurd."[1]

There are, quite naturally, different kinds of tragedy. Aristotle lists two general directions that the turn of fortune may take—either from good to bad or from bad to good.[2] In *The Sandbox* the turn seems to be the second kind, and Grandma goes from a state of querulousness and rebellion, mostly against her daughter, to one of insight, acceptance, and peace. Beyond the essential brevity of the action imitated in the play, the use of music, an equivalent of "Song" in Aristotle's list of the essential parts of tragedy (see *Poetics,* VI), gives *The Sandbox* a certain Grecian lyrical quality.

As mentioned earlier, Grandma acts as chorus in talking directly to the audience, as she provides the exposition about her past and complains about her daughter's treatment of her (149–52). In at least two speeches Mommy also plays this role of chorus, but Albee has her talk superciliously *"out over the audience,"* (148-49) when she complains about Grandma's throwing sand at her.[3] But more important than this incidental use of the characters for chorus effects is the way both the music and the Musician, as an actual character in the play, function as chorus.[4]

The Sandbox, Albee's second one-act tragedy, was well received. And although it may be argued that its frequent revivals have resulted from its relative ease and cheapness of production, its popularity, in our opinion, is also due to its enduring merit as a work of art.

CHAPTER 5

Excursion into Naturalism

I *Plot, Theme, Characters*

IF THE MISSION of serious literature is to *disturb*,[1] *The Death of Bessie Smith* certainly qualifies as a play that demands to be taken seriously; for it is the most *disturbing* play Albee has written, not excepting *Who's Afraid of Virginia Woolf?* It deserves something better than a flippant dismissal as mere propaganda for civil rights.

The play takes place "*in and around the city of Memphis, Tennessee*," and here Albee specifies the time exactly—"*afternoon and early evening, September 26, 1937*" (67). The front part of the stage represents "*the admissions room of a hospital*," where the main action occurs; but the back part has a slightly raised platform to depict with "*the most minimal suggestions of sets, the other scenes of the play . . .*" (68). Like *The Sandbox* "*the whole back wall is full of the sky*," varying widely in color and intensity from scene to scene (68). As the curtain goes up, the entire stage is dark against a "*hot blue*" sky (68).

When the lights come up, we hear music; and realize we are in "*the corner of a barroom*" (68). Bernie, a thin Negro, "*about forty*" (67), sits at a table drinking beer. Jack, a "*dark-skinned Negro, forty-five, bulky, with a deep voice and a mustache*," comes in; and they recognize each other (67). In this first of the eight scenes of the play, we learn that Jack is going to New York, "travelin'," as he says; and apparently he has knowledge of what he considers a "good thing" (70–72).

The second scene shifts to "*a screened-in porch*" at the home of the Nurse. The Father, a "*thin, balding white man, about fifty-five*," loafs, and alternately plays at being big politician and invalid; his daughter, the Nurse, is twenty-six, "*a southern white girl, full blown, dark or red-haired, pretty, with a wild laugh*"

(67). Complaining of a headache, he objects to the overloud phonographic music, "goddam nigger records," as he calls them. They argue about the family car—she, wanting him to drive her to work; he, saying he needs it.

She taunts him: "You going to drive down to the Democratic Club, and sit around with that bunch of loafers? You going to play big politician today? . . . You going to go down there with that bunch of bums . . . you going to sit down there and talk big, about how you and the mayor are like *this* . . . you going to pretend you're something more than you really are, which is nothing but . . . a hanger-on . . . a flunky . . ." (76–77).

He sneers back at her about her boyfriend: "Why don't you get your boy friend to drive you to work? . . . Why don't you get him to come by and pick you up, hunh? . . . Or is he only interested in driving you back here at night . . . when it's nice and dark; when it's plenty dark for messing around in his car? . . . I hear you; I hear you at night; I hear you gigglin' and carrying on out there in his car; I hear you!" (81–82). The scene ends on a note of mutual hate. We see both father and daughter as highly irritable, suspicious, mean—very mean—and as wanting to hurt each other to the utmost.

In the third scene Jack soliloquizes about his earlier meeting and talk with Bernie (downstairs in the barroom of the hotel) as he tries to wake up Bessie: "Hey . . . honey? Get your butt out of bed . . . wake up. C'mon; the goddam afternoon's half gone; we gotta get movin'" (83). Jack's soliloquy introduces us to Bessie's plight: she is a once-popular blues singer trying to make a comeback. In this scene, as in the two preceding ones, music plays in the background; and at the end of the scene the "*predominant*" sunset called for in the stage directions matches Bessie's decline from popularity and stardom. Also at the end of the scene, we hear Jack's voice, a car door slamming, and the motor gunning, as he says, "O.K.; here we go; we're on our way." Only then do we realize that Jack has actually maneuvered Bernie into supplying him and Bessie with a free ride north.

Looking at the first three scenes as a whole, we see they constitute an *ABA* pattern that introduces us to the two main parts of the societal conflict—the very slender plot concerning Bessie Smith's attempt to make a comeback and the dominant motif of racial bigotry, neurotic hatred, and various kinds of frustration, with the Nurse being the agent or prime mover of the action. Albee's object is to bring together these two lines of the plot by intertwining, or alternating, and then by ultimately bringing about an outright clash.

The first announcement of the theme of *racial discrimination within an institution dedicated to mercy* comes in scene four, one between the Nurse and the Orderly, "*a light-skinned Negro, twenty-eight, clean-shaven, trim, prim*" (67). The transition from the previous scene to the admissions room of the hospital is effected by a brief caricature of the mayor of Memphis, as presented by the Orderly:

> The mayor of Memphis! I went into his room and there he was . . . lying right there, flat on his belly . . . a cigar in his mouth . . . an unlit cigar in his mouth, chewing on it, chewing on a big, unlit cigar . . . shuffling a lot of papers in his hands, a pillow shoved up under his chest to give him some freedom for all those papers . . . and I came in, and I said: Good afternoon, Your Honor . . . and he swung his face 'round and he looked at me and he shouted: My ass hurts, you get the hell out of here! (86)

The Nurse "*laughs freely*" and says, "His Honor has got his ass in a sling, and that's for sure." The Orderly explains that he got out, "left very quickly," "closed the door fast." The Nurse then goes on:

> The mayor and his hemorrhoids . . . the mayor's late hemorrhoids . . . are a matter of deep concern to this institution, for the mayor built this hospital; the mayor is here with his ass in a sling, and the seat of government is now in Room 206 . . . so you be nice and respectful. (*Laughs*) There is a man two rooms down who walked in here last night after you went off . . . that man walked in here with his hands over his gut to keep his insides from spilling right out on this desk . . . and that man may live, or he may not live, and the wagers are heavy that he will not live . . . but we are not one bit more concerned for that man than we are for His Honor . . . no sir. (86–87)

When the Orderly remonstrates with her for her false code of values, she retorts: "Now it's true that the poor man lying up there with his guts coming out could be a nigger for all the attention he'd get if His Honor should start shouting for something . . . he could be on the operating table . . . and they'd drop his insides right on the floor and come running if the mayor should want his cigar lit.... But that is the way things *are*. Those are facts. You had better acquaint yourself with some realities" (88).

She also attacks the Orderly for using big words, like *condone* and *contempt*, as if a colored person had no right to an educated vocabulary (87). In the ensuing conversation, which dates the play as well as her prejudice, the Nurse makes a vicious attack on the Roosevelts, saying: "Would you like me to recite some verse for you? Here is a little poem: 'You kiss the niggers and I'll kiss the Jews and we'll stay in the White House as long as we choose.' And that... according to what I am told is what Mr. and Mrs. Roosevelt sit at the breakfast table and sing to each other over their orange juice, right in the White House" (89–90).

When the Orderly replies that there are "some people who believe in action" rather than in political promises, she turns an eye of death upon him and says: "You been listening to the great white doctor again... that big, good-looking blond intern you *admire* so much because he is so liberal-thinking, eh? My suitor? (*Laughs*) ... my very own white knight, who is wasting his time patching up decent folk right here when there is dying going on in Spain. (*Exaggerated*) Oh, there is dying in Spain. And he is held here! That's who you have been listening to" (91).

Another function of scene four is to characterize the Intern, already talked about in the second scene as a type of liberal thinker who is caught in a dilemma: on the one hand, he has to choose between the sexual attraction of the Nurse and perfunctory fulfillment of his hospital residence requirement and, on the other, his conviction that his services are really needed in the Spanish War (between Fascist Franco and the Communists). His failure to resolve this dilemma makes his situation hopelessly absurd. His professional conscience tells him that he is wasting his time by remaining where he is and by conforming to the demands of society, but the Nurse's sexual charm paralyzes his will and transforms him into a ridiculous figure of inaction.

But, if the Intern is trapped in a dilemma of this kind, the meshes of an even more absurd situation tangle and confuse the Orderly's thought processes; for he has the problem of saying "yes'm" to everything the Nurse says in order to keep his job (91); at the same time, his real sympathies lie with the socially liberating views of the Intern. In the talk between the Nurse and the Orderly that follows, it comes out that the Orderly's uncle had been "run down by a truck full of state police," which, as she says, "the Governor called out because of the rioting . . . and that arson! Action! That was a fine bunch of action. Is that what you mean? Is that what you get him off in a corner and get him to talk about . . . and pretend you're interested? Listen, boy . . . if you're going to get yourself in with those folks, you'd better. . . ."

To the Orderly's quick denial that he is mixed up with "any folks," she forcefully reminds him that to keep his "good job" he must not only keep his ears and "mouth closed tight" but also "keep walking a real tight line here, and . . . and at night (*She begins to giggle*) . . . and at night, if you want to, on your own time . . . at night you keep right on putting that bleach on your hands and your neck and your face. . . ." When he indignantly denies doing this and intimates that he finds her talk offensive, she rants away at him again:

> . . . you are so mixed up! You are going to be one funny sight. You, over there in a corner playing up to him . . . well, boy, you are going to be one funny sight come the millennium . . . The great black mob marching down the street, banners in the air . . . that great black mob . . . and you right there in the middle, your bleached-out, snowy white face in the middle of the pack like that . . . (*She breaks down in laughter*) . . . oh . . . oh, my . . . oh. I tell you, that will be quite a sight. (93–94)

After calling him "a genuine little ass-licker," she continues with malicious solicitude: "Tell me, boy . . . is it true that you have Uncle Tom'd yourself right out of the bosom of your family . . . right out of your circle of acquaintances? Is it true, young man, that you are now an inhabitant of no-man's-land, on the one side shunned and disowned by your brethren, and on the other an object of contempt and derision to your betters? Is that your problem, son?" (95). The Orderly is educated, to a degree at least (he uses big words that she doesn't understand); but education, instead of providing a richer and more expansive life, ironically only isolates him from his own people. Further factors in his isolation are his light color and his "Uncle Tom" qualities—qualities which, ironically, she demands of him, as Sylvia Bowman has pointed out.

At the end of the scene the Nurse advises the Orderly to go "up to New York City, where nobody's any better than anybody else.... But before you do anything like that, you run on downstairs and get me a pack of cigarettes" (95). When he seems about to speak up, he says "Yes'm" and dutifully departs after the cigarettes. After he leaves, she mimicks him, saying, "Yes'm ... yes'm ... ha, ha, ha! You white niggers kill me" (96).

The fifth scene is very short in comparison with the one preceding it. It introduces a new character, the Second Nurse, and adds to the complication by presenting her at the admissions desk of a second hospital—represented theatrically by a raised platform at the back of the stage. The first Nurse is seated at a desk in the first hospital—at the front of the stage. Both nurses are bored—the gossipy telephone conversation between them is meaningless. "What did you call for?" asks the Second Nurse. "I didn't call *for* anything," replies the first Nurse. "I (*Shrugs*) just called" (97).

The lights dim, and the stage directions call for music and car sounds. We hear Jack talking to Bessie: "(*Laughs*) I tell you, honey, he didn't like that. No, sir, he didn't. You comfortable, honey. Hunh? You just lean back and enjoy the ride, baby; we're makin' good time. Yes, we are makin'... WATCH OUT! WATCH ... (*Sound of crash.... Silence*) Honey ... baby ... we have crashed ... you all right?... BESSIE! BESSIE!" (97). When lights and music come up again on the two nurses, one in each hospital, they are still gossiping on the telephone—about the mayor and his wife; and their languid, bored telephone conversation is interrupted in the first hospital by the entrance of the Intern whom the first Nurse calls "lover boy" (98).

The efficiency of these two so-called institutions of mercy with their indolent nurses comes under direct fire during this scene. One of the hospitals is Mercy Hospital, and the two nurses idly bat the word *mercy* around two or three times at the start of the scene. The crashing auto sounds against the lazy and inefficient nurses' chit-chat, symbolically dramatizing the racial conflict. Actually, this scene prepares the audience for the culminating absurdity of the eighth and last scene of the play.

Scene six is long, possibly overlong. (It is just slightly less long than the final eighth scene.) The Intern, who has now entered, proceeds to proposition the Nurse, who is now in a slightly more receptive mood than when they had parted. He gives vent to his yearning for sex in a rather strained geometrical metaphor, and she plays along with him. He offers to marry her; she counters that the Orderly, the "nigger," as she calls him, earns more than his own paltry forty-six dollars a month as Intern—"and by a *lot*" (106). "Why don't you just ask that nigger to marry you?" he shoots back at her; and she tries to burn him with her cigarette, which, incidentally, she had borrowed from him (101, 107). Then she apologizes, calls him "honey," and offers a different proposition, hinting broadly that he ought to butter up the mayor to further his medical career.

The Intern apparently cannot bring himself to do this. He would "like to get away" to Spain where his services are really needed, where over half a million civilians have been killed, and where more are constantly dying for lack of doctors. Deeply aware of the absurdity of his position (he is merely putting in time working out his internship while his services are desperately needed in the Spanish War), he says: "... you listen to me. If I could... if I could bandage the arm of one person... if I could be over there right this minute... you could take the city of Memphis... you could take the whole state... and *don't you forget I was born here*... you could take the whole goddam state..." (110–11, my italics).

She threatens to "tell the mayor about the way you feel," adding that this dignitary would undoubtedly be delighted to help him on his way. "He'd set you out, all right," she says, "he'd set you right out on your *butt*!" (111). She tells him to "walk a straight line" and do his job. Then, turning suddenly coy, she offers to let him drive her home that night in his "beat-up Chevvy" (112).

The audience's notion of their passionate petting (mentioned earlier by her father) is here reinforced when the Intern describes the "ritual" which, he says, always stops short of sexual intercourse with her hasty departure after tantalizing preliminaries. But he ruins their short-lived rapport when he says: "I look forward to this ritual because of how it sets me apart from other men... because I am probably the only white man under sixty in two counties who has *not* had the pleasure of..." (112–13). At this statement she rages, calls him a liar, filth, a "no-account mother-grabbing son of a nigger!" and swears to "get" him, insisting (more to spite him than anything else) that he drive her home that night, "see me to my *door* . . . be my gallant." "We will have things between us a little bit the way I am told things *used* to be," she says. "You will *court* me, boy, and you will do it right!" (115–16). He stares at her. "You impress me," he says finally. "No matter what else, I've got to admit that" (116). She laughs wildly to music and a fadeout as the scene ends.

This long middle part of the plot (scenes four, five, and six) develops the societal conflict, first, by introducing the Orderly as the direct or immediate butt of the Nurse's white supremacist attack (scene four). Then in scene five, through the phone call between the two nurses in different hospitals and through the interrupting crash of Jack's car carrying Bessie, Albee draws the two strings of his plot closer together. In scene six, the unsuccessful proposition of the Intern to the Nurse and his slur on her reputation provide a motive for her plan to revenge herself on him. Briefly, this middle section of the plot prepares us for the third and culminating section: the advent of Jack and Bessie at the two different hospitals—respectively, in scenes seven and eight.

As the lights come up in scene seven on the Second Nurse at the other hospital, Jack rushes in, announcing an emergency, explaining that he has an injured woman in his car outside. To which the Second Nurse retorts: "Yeah? Is that so? Well, you sit down and wait. . . . You go over there and sit down and wait a while." When he remonstrates that the woman is badly hurt and needs immediate help, she shouts back, "YOU COOL YOUR HEELS!" (117). When Jack explains "I got Bessie Smith out in that car there . . . ," the Second Nurse yells, "I DON'T CARE WHO YOU GOT OUT THERE, NIGGER. YOU COOL YOUR HEELS!" (117).

What Albee calls "SCENE EIGHT" actually is composed of six smaller scenes, or sections (in the strict sense of a scene's being a new grouping of characters on the stage). The first of these takes us back to the first hospital with the Nurse and the Intern and shows the Orderly returning with the cigarettes he had been sent for. When the Intern asks if it is now her plan to send him for coffee, she, "*smiling wickedly,*" informs him that she thinks she would like to keep them both jumping. Amid sexual innuendoes (119), he moves off to do her bidding.

In the door he stops to deliver what he calls a "lovely thought": the prospect of her accidentally slipping and cutting herself with the stiletto she uses for a letter opener, her running to him for help during this emergency, and his deliberately watching her bleed to death. Actually, this speech prepares the audience for what really happens to Bessie Smith later on; but when the Intern utters it, we are less aware of its function as preparation than as an expression of his hatred because of sexual frustration. She, of course, hates him even more; she threatens to stab him on the spot and vows, after he is gone, that she will take care of him—to crack the whip over him now that she has a slight edge of power because he had insulted her by impugning her morals.

The Nurse's own sexual frustration is presented most strongly in the second small part of "SCENE EIGHT." In this important scene she confuses her feeling for her father, an avowed admirer of Francisco Franco, with her attraction (at least sexually) for the Intern and (at least unconsciously) for the colored Orderly. This triple confusion deserves a little analysis. It will be remembered that the Nurse had left home that morning hating her father. Now, however, in her agitated state, or love-hate for the Intern, she automatically sides with her father; for his views on the Spanish Civil War are exactly opposite to those of the Intern. I say *love-hate* advisedly, because in her soliloquy—it can be called that because she so pointedly ignores the existence or presence of the Orderly—her unconscious sexual attraction (I hesitate to call it *love*) breaks through the meanness of her consciousness as she tells the Orderly that he and she are "practically engaged, going to be married." She is thinking of the Intern (see 123) as she talks to the Orderly but ignores his existence.

At the same time, she is playing a mean, scornful game with the Orderly. She enjoys his befuddlement as well as the exercise of her power over him—for this is white supremacy in action, a situation where stupidity holds the whiphand over intelligence since the Orderly is far brighter than she is—and unconsciously expresses her attraction to the Negro and her own self-hatred. Her last speech reaches its climax in a passionate outcry against the system of white supremacy that she has been defending.

As though nature itself were outraged and protesting, she

cries: "I am sick of everything in this hot, stupid, fly-ridden *world.* I am sick of the disparity between things as they are, and as they should be! . . . I am tired . . . I am tired of the truth . . . and I am tired of lying about the truth . . . I am tired of my skin . . . I WANT OUT!" (124–25). At the same time, however, she is lucid enough to distinguish between the Orderly and the Intern: "I am sick of the sight of *you* [the Orderly] . . . the *thought* of you makes me *itch.* . . . I am sick of *him* [the Intern]" (124).

But she is nevertheless so shaken by this breakdown, this completely honest outburst of her true feelings, that we feel it quite appropriate when the Orderly suggests that she go into the emergency room and lie down. As he approaches her to help her, she misinterprets his movement as a sexual overture, or an attack; and she warns him, "Keep away from me" (125). This reaction shows quite clearly that she is thinking of him as a lover, however unconsciously or ambivalently.

Whatever her true feelings may have been, or what she might have done about them, we are saved from knowing; for just then Jack bursts into the admissions room of the hospital. According to the stage directions, he is "*drunk, shocked, frightened*" (125), and he is also "*very confused*" (126) because neither the Orderly nor the Nurse seems to know why he is there. They simply cannot comprehend that, being of his color, he should ever have the temerity to think of bringing a colored woman—no matter how badly injured—to this hospital reserved exclusively for white people. His defiance in the face of their refusal to accept Bessie is interrupted by the reappearance of the Intern, which marks the beginning of the fourth part.

The Intern takes the Orderly outside with him to investigate Bessie's injuries—despite the threats of the Nurse to "fix" him. After they go out, in part five, the Nurse talks to Jack, who describes for her (and the audience) the details of the accident. She coldly listens to his story, including his account of Bessie's serious injuries and the refusal of the Second Nurse, at the other white hospital, to admit Bessie as a patient because of Jim Crow laws. All the Nurse's small mentality can glean from Jack's entire narration is that he "drove away from an accident" (136). She feels it her duty to report him to the police for doing so; for it never occurs to her that, in any conflict between preserving either the law or human life, life should have any consideration.

In the sixth and last part of "SCENE EIGHT" the Intern returns inside after discovering that Bessie is dead. When the Nurse tells the Intern that Jack drove away from the scene of an accident, he tells her to shut up. He is more interested in another feature of the case: "When you brought this woman *here* . . . when you drove up *here* . . . when you brought this woman *here* . . . DID YOU KNOW SHE WAS DEAD?" (135). To this query Jack replies, "Yes . . . I knew she was dead. She died on the way here." Then the Intern explodes: "WHAT DID YOU EXPECT ME TO DO? WHAT WAS I SUPPOSED TO DO?" (136).

The Nurse taunts him, saying that he was supposed to bring the "dead nigger lady" back to life and that he is now "finished"; for she, too, plans to "sing," although in a different sense of the word. And she collapses into hysteria of laughter that is a tuneless singing which is "*almost keening.*" To bring her out of this state, he slaps her; she freezes, "*with her hand to her face where he hit her*" (136). While he backs to the rear door, the Orderly makes this absurd comment: "I never heard of such a thing . . . bringing a dead woman here like that . . . I don't know what people can be thinking of sometimes . . ." (136). And with this statement he personifies under pressure the Nurse's earlier advice to him: "You just jump to it and say what you think people want to hear . . . you be both sides of the coin" (122). The Intern goes out; "*the great sunset blazes*" (137) as music comes up and the curtain rings down.

II *The Final Effect*

The Intern's final explosion matches the breakdown of the Nurse just before Jack enters the admissions room. This explosion is compounded of various frustrations—sexual, professional, and racial. Like the Nurse's, his feeling toward the object of his affection may best be described as an ambivalent combination of love and hate. Inexperienced in the gentle art of receiving corpses at the hospital door, he also suffers from professional frustration—he is enough of a doctor to want to keep patients alive. But he also belongs to the established society, and he knows very well what happens to those who violate the mores of white supremacy. Once having had the courage to violate these mores in a moment of defiance in the war between the sexes, he discovers, to his intense mortification, that the courage of his heroic violation has evaporated, as has his career (in this particular place) because of his willingness to treat Bessie Smith.

The audience, unlike the Intern, sees more of Albee's *end*, or *purpose*, because it can take a slightly more disinterested view of the young doctor's frustrations. If the Intern is the protagonist and if the Nurse is the antagonist—since between and around them the conflict mostly rages—the final effect of the play can hardly be considered the arousal and purgation of Aristotelian *pity* and *fear*, because these emotions are usually felt only for the protagonist. We may pity the Intern for his temporarily blasted career, and we may fear for him because he is a man like ourselves; but this pity and fear do not seem to constitute the principal emotional effects of the play. Rather, the effect consists of *anger* or *indignation* at the general situation—savage hatred of the injustice caused by white supremacy and the vicious Jim Crow laws that can create a social system in which the mayor of Memphis' hemorrhoids become objects of tender concern while the life of another human being bleeds into nothingness.

For this reason the *kind* of play Albee has written seems to be basically a *rhetorical* (or persuasive) one. Its function is to arouse indignation at certain forms of social injustice in a large and an important area of the country. The play implicitly persuades us that we must, in the name of basic humanity, change mores that create or permit this kind of injustice in our democracy. Clearly a thesis play, one of strong social protest, it calls our attention to a horrible crime of our time—racial discrimination in so-called institutions of mercy.[2] The play marks Albee's deep concern as a social critic of American culture, his attempt to speak out bravely on a subject regarded by many more financially successful playwrights at that time as too dangerous to handle.

But how can we possibly understand the general and widespread problem of white supremacy and racial discrimination if we neglect probing into the fundamental, existential state of sexual frustration (and its explosive consequences) in the lives of individual persons? I should like to compare the tone of the ending with that of Sartre's *No Exit*, where, because of the hellish inextricability of the situation, all of the characters more or less abandon all hope. Such a resolution cannot be called *tragedy*, *comedy,* or *tragi-comedy.* Apart from the rhetorical character already mentioned, there is *tragedy,* certainly—but it is a pervasive tragedy and not one limited to a single character as in the older Greek drama of Aeschylus, Sophocles, and Euripides or in such modern tragedies as those of Tennessee Williams and Arthur Miller.

In its essential spirit and technique *Bessie Smith* also closely resembles Sartre's *The Respectful Prostitute,* in which sex and race are also treated. I cannot recall that any of the regular drama critics brought these resemblances to Sartre to the attention of readers.[3]

CHAPTER 6

Expressionistic Satire

ALTHOUGH Albee's subtitle to *The American Dream** is *A Play in One Scene,* the play really has eleven scenes or regroupings of characters.[1] These scenes fall into three major parts: one to four, inclusively, deal with the conflict between Mommy and Grandma (Mommy wants to put Grandma away, presumably in a nursing home); five to seven present the visit of Mrs. Barker, a colleague club lady of Mommy's who had once worked for the Bye-Bye Adoption Service, from whom Mommy and Daddy had acquired an "unsatisfactory" child; eight to eleven describe the arrival of the handsome young man, "The American Dream" as he is called, and tell how Grandma uses him to foil Mommy's plan to have her placed in a nursing home.

The trio of central characters bears close resemblance to the Mommy, Daddy, and Grandma of *The Sandbox.* The general situation—the scheme to dispose of Grandma and the frustration of this plan by the clever Grandma who acts in consort with the muscular young man—is also quite similar to that of *The Sandbox.* But that is about as far as meaningful comparisons can be carried; for while *The Sandbox* represents a rather special kind of *tragedy, The American Dream* obviously falls into the general category of *satire,* notwithstanding Albee's reference to it in his preface as a "comedy."[2]

The author provides a clue to consideration of *satire* in his statement that "The play is an examination of the American Scene, an attack on the substitution of artificial for real values in our society . . . a stand against the fiction that everything in this slipping land of ours is peachy-keen" (8). A random list of specific artificial values under fire includes the following:

*Used by permission of Coward-McCann, Inc., from THE AMERICAN DREAM by Edward Albee; © 1961 by Edward Albee.

1. The importance of distinctive dress at any cost.
2. *Power* as a substitute for *love* in family life.
3. *Sex* as a substitute for love.
4. The importance of money in marriage—female parasitism.
5. The paramount importance of firmness, decisiveness, and masculinity in the American male.
6. Institutionalization of old people as the only efficient method of treating them.
7. Personal comfort before public duty.
8. The exaggerated importance of TV.
9. Social climbing.
10. Worship of the body beautiful and athleticism.

I *Mommy's Plan for Grandma*

In the first scene Mommy and Daddy sit in armchairs in the living room of their apartment. They are expecting visitors, who are late, and this tardiness disturbs them. Meanwhile, their conversation ranges from complaints about things out of order in their apartment to a history of how Mommy exchanged a new beige-colored hat after her club chairman, Mrs. Barker, had said it was wheat-colored. Daddy opines that it may have been the same hat "they tried to sell you before." "Well, of course it was!" exclaims Mommy. But the important thing, as she brings out, is that "You [Daddy] can't get satisfaction." She tells Daddy, "just try. I can get satisfaction, but you can't" (16). Certainly part of the function of this scene is to present Mommy as representative of American female dictatorship in the home.[3]

At the end of this first scene they talk about Grandma, who is being driven to tears because the toilet doesn't work. Mommy says Grandma is becoming "feeble-headed" (17). Then, at the beginning of scene two, Grandma walks on stage, carrying a great load of boxes, as though preparing to move out. She is crotchety and perverse in her snappy retorts to Mommy and Daddy, but she enlists the sympathy of the audience by her opposition to Mommy's cruel way of treating and talking to her and also by her comments on old people, which show insight and intelligence.

When Grandma goes out after more boxes (scene three), Mommy reminisces with Daddy about her childhood, revealing unwittingly her own selfishness and deceit but her mother's (Grandma's) capacity for self-sacrifice. In this conversation she also reveals quite shamelessly that she had married Daddy for his money: "You can't live off people. I can live off you because I married you.... I have a right to live off of you because I married you, and because I used to let you get on top of me and bump your uglies; and I have a right to all your money when you die" (22–23). Then she shares with him her plan to put Grandma in a nursing home.

When Grandma comes back in with more boxes (scene four), she learns of their plan to put her away. Apparently Mommy had talked of it before, and the old lady senses that they are expecting someone to come take her away. Although Daddy is somewhat reluctant to have Grandma carried off, Mommy hypocritically flatters him into thinking the decision to do so was his and that he had been "firm... masculine and decisive" in making it (30). Although she deceives him and wins him over to her side, she does not do so before Grandma has got in a few good licks of her own about her daughter's nauseating character as a child: "She was a tramp and a trollop and a trull to boot, and she's no better now.... When she was no more than eight years old she used to climb up on my lap and say, in a sickening little voice, "when I gwo up, I'm going to mahwy a wich old man; I'm going to set my wittle were end right down in a tub o' butter, that's what I'm going to do.' And I warned you, Daddy; I told you to stay away from her type" (25).

When the doorbell rings, Daddy answers it, thinking to admit the "van" men to cart Grandma off to some kind of institution for the aged. But to his surprise, Mrs. Barker, a certain type of professional clubwoman, comes in (35, 50–51). Wearing a hat exactly like Mommy's new one, she insists it is "cream"-colored instead of *beige* and illogically carries her point by reminding Mommy that she (not Mommy) is president of their woman's club. In the ensuing long scene five (32–52), she makes herself completely comfortable, going so far as to take off her dress (a theatrical device whereby Albee satirizes the tendency of American women to display their sexual power by public exposure) and thereby to overstimulate Daddy (38).

In general, this scene increases the conflict and hostility between Mommy and Grandma. At the end of it, Mommy commands Daddy to smash the tubes of Grandma's television because Grandma has contradicted her. Wearily, he goes to do her bidding.

After he is gone, Grandma commits another "sin" by refusing to get Mrs. Barker a glass of water. "Go get it yourself," she says. "I quit" (54). To which Mommy replies, "Now, you be a good Grandma, or you know what will happen to you. You'll be taken away in a van" (54). When Grandma answers that she is not frightened by this threat, Mommy says she will punish her by hiding her teeth. At the end of this sixth scene, Mommy goes to get the water for Mrs. Barker.

When she is alone with Mrs. Barker (scene seven), Grandma takes the opportunity to expose a little more of the past family life of Mommy and Daddy, reminding Mrs. Barker of her previous visit (Mrs. Barker claims she can't remember it). The reason for her lapse of memory, we judge, is her preoccupation with club activities (50, 51).

> MRS. BARKER: . . . they say I was here before.
> GRANDMA: Well, you were. You weren't *here,* exactly, because we've moved around a lot, from one apartment to another, up and down the social ladder like mice, if you like similes. (55)

This earlier visit of Mrs. Barker's had been connected with her work as a representative of the Bye-Bye Adoption Service and with Mommy and Daddy's adoption of a child.

According to Grandma, Mommy and Daddy had killed the child, dismembering it little by little in the most gruesome fashion for everything it did that was *natural;* in short, they had killed it for its failure to develop according to their own artificial values.[4] "Well," Grandma concludes, "it finally up and died; and you can imagine how *that* made them feel, their having paid for it, and all. So, they called up the lady who sold them the bumble in the first place and told her to come right over to their apartment. They wanted satisfaction; they wanted their money back. That's what they wanted. . . . How do you like *them* apples?" (62–63).

Gradually it becomes clear to stupid Mrs. Barker that she may have been the woman who sold them the "bumble," but she says she'll "have to think about it . . . mull it" (67). Accordingly, she goes off to get the glass of water Mommy has as yet failed to bring her, but her failure represents a ruse to separate Mrs. Barker from Grandma before Grandma tells her something Mommy doesn't want her to know.

II *Grandma's Plan for Mommy*

Scene eight marks the arrival of the unemployed Young Man, who is looking for work (72). (There is so much that needs fixing in the apartment that his otherwise unexplained appearance on the scene does not seriously violate probability.) When Grandma mistakes him for the van man—"Are you come to take me away?" (68)—he doesn't know what she is talking about. As she looks him over, she admires his muscles, his youth, his profile; and she suggests he ought to be in the movies, a remark he has heard before. The Young Man, empty-headed enough to go along with her enraptured admiration, says of his face, "It's quite good, isn't it? Clean-cut, midwest farm boy type, almost insultingly good-looking in a typically American way. Good profile, straight nose, honest eyes, wonderful smile. . . ." "Yup," rejoins Grandma, "Boy, you know what you are, don't you? You're the American Dream, that's what you are. All those other people, they don't know what they're talking about. You . . . *you* are the American Dream" (70).

True to his character as American Dream, the Young Man will "do almost anything for money" (72). Grandma begins to think that there just possibly might be something he could do around there; but, first, she lets him in on a secret. She had won a twenty-five-thousand-dollar cake-baking contest under the pseudonym of Uncle Henry, her entry being called "Uncle Henry's Day-Old Cake" (74). "All I did was go out and get a store-bought cake," she explains, "and keep it around for a while and then slip it in, unbeknownst to anybody . . . how do you like them apples?"

He then tells her his secret: the reason he will do almost anything for money is that he really has "no talents at all, except what you see—my person; my body, my face. In every other way I am incomplete . . ." (76). More particularly, he suffers an awful sense of incompleteness because of the absence of his identical twin brother[5] from whom he was "torn apart," in babyhood apparently. This traumatic experience makes him incapable of loving. "I no longer have the capacity to feel anything," he says. "I have no emotions. I have been drained, torn asunder . . . disembowelled. I have, now, only my person . . . my body, my face. I use what I have" (78). Deeply affected by his tale, Grandma decides to help him—and herself. When they hear Mrs. Barker returning, Grandma warns him he must "play it by ear" if he wants a paying job (79).

When Mrs. Barker comes in, Grandma fabricates by introducing the Young Man to her as "the van man" (80), asking him to carry her boxes of belongings outside (81–82). She then takes Mrs. Barker into her confidence. Together they agree to Grandma's twofold plan: first, to pass off the Young Man as "the van man;" second, to substitute him for the previous "unsatisfactory" child (who, we gather, was the young man's aforementioned identical twin brother). Thus Grandma plans to foil Mommy's scheme to have her incarcerated in an institution for the aged. The agreement to this plan is the substance (or function) of scene nine. And the last two scenes (ten and eleven) work out the details of this action.

Mommy, coming on stage in scene ten, registers surprise at finding Grandma missing; for she had not, apparently, however much she had talked of it, completed her scheme to call the van people. But in scene eleven her state of hypocritical tearfulness is dissipated by Mrs. Barker, who assures her that she herself saw the van people take Grandma off. Moreover, Mommy is much attracted to the handsome, muscular Young Man whose presence in the household as a substitute for Grandma (and for the previous "unsatisfactory" child) she accepts with alacrity. In an interesting bit of stage business she circles the Young Man, "*feeling his arms, poking him,*" and saying "Yes, sir! Yes, siree! Now this is more like it. Now this is a great deal more like it! Daddy! Come see. Come see if this isn't a great deal more like it." When Daddy readily agrees that "it does look a great deal more like it" (89–90), they all decide to celebrate. From the bottom of her false heart Mommy thanks Mrs. Barker, and they all drink to "satisfaction." Triumphantly Mommy exclaims: "Who says you can't get satisfaction these days!" (92).

In character, Mrs. Barker inanely remarks on the "dreadful sauterne"; and Mommy inanely says "Yes, isn't it?" (92). Then, slightly under the influence of the wine, she sidles up to the

Young Man, promising to tell him all about the other child after Mrs. Barker has gone—"maybe later tonight." As he replies, "that would be very nice," she begins to sense something vaguely familiar about him (93).

Playing the chorus to this absurd action, Grandma wraps up the play with a speech directed to the audience, a speech which maintains the wonderfully satiric tone of the play as a whole to the very end: "Well, I guess that just about wraps it up. I mean, for better or worse, this is a comedy, and I don't think we'd better go any further. No, definitely not. So, let's leave things as they are right now . . . while everybody's got what he wants . . . or everybody's got what he thinks he wants. Good night, dears" (93).

CHAPTER 7

Battle of the Sexes—New Style

WITH *Who's Afraid of Virginia Woolf?* Albee achieved a more or less secure position for himself in the history of modern American drama. His first Broadway production, this long, three-act play rapidly developed into a box-office success of major proportions. Historically, the play was important for another reason: it marked some kind of new development on a popular Elizabethan theme of war between the sexes, such as we find in *The Taming of the Shrew* and in the merry war between Beatrice and Benedick in *Much Ado About Nothing* of Shakespeare.

I *The Games of the Play*

The first act of the play, entitled "Fun and Games," begins with a sharp quarrel between Martha and George. The time is two o'clock on Sunday morning, and they have just returned from a Saturday night drinking party at Martha's father's house. (Martha's father is president of the small New England college in which George is an associate professor of history.) The stage is dark. We hear a crash against the front door, Martha's laughter, and (as the lights switch on) her opening speech, a protracted oath, "*Jesus* . . . H. Christ," and George's "Shhhhhh"—all of which seems to indicate some degree of inebriety.[1] Martha's gaze roves the room; and then, imitating Bette Davis, she brays out, "What a dump. Hey, what's that from? 'What a dump!' " (3). With these words the quarrel begins, and it speedily rises to a fairly intense pitch to tell the audience that all is not well with this particular marriage.

The quarrel between Martha and George about identification of the Bette Davis movie prepares us for the revelation we receive at the end of the act, because the situation of Bette Davis in the movie bears some resemblance to that of Martha in real life. When George cannot identify the movie, Martha—with laborious sarcasm—recalls for him details of Bette Davis's behavior in it:

> she comes home with the groceries, and she walks into the modest living room of the modest cottage modest Joseph Cotten has set her up in. . . .
>
> GEORGE: Are they married?
>
> MARTHA: Yes, They're married. To each other. Cluck! And she comes in, and she looks around, and she puts her groceries down, and she says, "What a dump!"
>
> GEORGE: (*Pause*) Oh.
>
> MARTHA: (*Pause*) She's discontent. (6)

Martha, as it turns out, is also discontented in marriage; furthermore, she is suffering from a long-standing psychological repression of an unsolved problem that the alcoholic intoxication and the consequent events of the play in the third act eventually flush out of deep hiding in the labyrinth of her subconsciousness. Other aspects of her marital "discontent" come out with references to the couple's relations with her father and her criticisms of George's failure ever to "*do* anything." "You never *do* anything," she tells him; "you never *mix*. You just sit around and *talk*" (7). He retorts, "What do you want me to do? Do you want me to act like you? Do you want me to go around all night *braying* at everybody, the way you do?" And the squabble continues in full force until Martha asks for a *drink*, not a "nightcap," as she informs him that guests are coming.

The second part of the first scene begins at this point. Martha explains that they had already met the invited couple that night at her father's party—"He's in the math department . . . about thirty, blond, and . . . good looking" (9). "His wife's a mousey little type, without any hips or anything" (10). George wants to know why they are coming at this time of the morning, to which Martha in her befuddled obstinacy can only reply, "Because Daddy said we should be nice to them" (10).

As the quarrel continues, George objects to Martha's "springing things" on him all the time. Martha attempts making up to him; she tries to amuse him by repeating the song sung earlier at the party, "Who's afraid of Virginia Woolf, Virginia Woolf,

Virginia Woolf," to the tune of "Here We Go Round the Mulberry Bush." When she dislikes the way he now responds to hearing it, she continues her ugly, quarrelsome talk and behavior, at one moment saying he makes her "puke," at the next demanding he put more ice in her drink and kiss her.

Martha obviously enjoys provoking George, and he is spirited enough and sufficiently under the influence of alcohol to give as murderously as he receives. She threatens to divorce him: "I swear . . . if you existed I'd divorce you." Arrogantly, she orders him to answer the door bell. Although he at first refuses, he finally concedes, but only after wringing out of her a more or less tacit agreement not to talk about "the kid"—a point that Albee stresses (18–19). Their quarrel again follows an upward curve, and just as she shouts a vulgar command at the top of her lungs, he flings open the door to the guests, Nick and Honey, who receive the full force of this obscenity as their welcome. For a brief moment they stand in silence, framed by the door entrance.

The appearance of Nick and Honey marks the beginning of the second scene and we immediately gain greater insight into the character of George. For when he says, "Ahhhhhhhhhh!" Albee indicates the following stage direction: "(*Ostensibly a pleased recognition of Honey and Nick, but really satisfaction at having Martha's explosion overheard*)" (19). Somewhat hesitantly, Nick and Honey come in to join the party. George and Martha now intersperse cutting remarks to each other with amiable chit-chat with which they from time to time attempt to hide their hostilities.

The function of this scene as a whole is characterization. George shows his intellectual superiority by joshing Nick with clichés when the latter attempts to say something meaningful about an abstract painting hanging on the wall. The painting had been done by "some Greek with a mustache Martha attacked one night in . . .," according to George (21). Incidental as the point may seem, it nonetheless tends to characterize Martha's aggressiveness toward men and to prepare us for her later aggressive action toward Nick. More drinks are passed around, and the guests join in singing the song about Virginia Woolf.

Honey and Nick, who are new to the faculty, attempt to flatter

Martha by praising her father:

> HONEY (*To Martha*): And your father! Oh! He is so marvelous!
> NICK (*As above*) [attempting enthusiasm]: Yes . . . yes, he is.
> HONEY: Oh, I tell you.
> MARTHA: (*Genuinely proud*): He's quite a guy, isn't he? Quite a guy.
> GEORGE: (*At Nick*): And you'd better believe it!
> HONEY (*Admonishing George*): Ohhhhhhhhh! He's a wonderful man.
> GEORGE: I'm not trying to tear him down. He's a God, we all know that.
> MARTHA: You lay off my father!
>
> ....
>
> MARTHA: Well, *Daddy* knows how to run things.
> NICK (*not enough enthusiasm*): He's a remarkable man.
> MARTHA: You bet your sweet life.
> GEORGE: (*To Nick . . . a confidence, but not whispered*): Let me tell you a secret, baby. There are easier things in the world, if you happen to be teaching at a university, there are easier things than being married to the daughter of the president of that university. There are easier things in this world. (26–27)

At the end of the scene, when Martha escorts Honey to the ladies' room, George reminds his wife not to talk about the "you-know-what [their imaginary child]." Martha replies with surprising vehemence, "I'll talk about any goddam thing I want to . . . Any goddam thing I want to!" (29–30). Left alone, George and Nick talk in the third scene about George's "dashed hopes and good intentions" (32) and about Martha's father. They also discuss various other topics—such as the length of time George has been at the "small college," where, as he says, "musical beds is the faculty sport," and their respective ages and weights as well as those of their wives.

George is intellectually superior to all other characters, definitely strongly interested in Martha, and also keenly interested in continuing their love-hate, their battle of the sexes, the fun and games of their "exercising," their "walking what's left of our wits," as he calls their quarrel (35–36). Beyond developing the characterization, this scene presents an exposition by George of his failure to rise in the ranks of the college administration: "I *did* run the History Department, for four years, during the war, but that was because everybody was away. Then . . . everybody came back . . . because nobody got killed. That's New England for you. Isn't that amazing? Not one single man in this whole place got his head shot off. That's pretty irrational. (*Broods*) Your wife *doesn't* have any hips . . . has she . . . does she?" (38–39).

Then, after staring up at the ceiling and wondering what the women are doing up there, he goes on:

> Not one son-of-a-bitch got killed. Of course, nobody bombed Washington. No . . . that's not fair. You have any kids?
>
> NICK: Uh . . . no . . . not yet. (*Pause*) You?
>
> GEORGE (*A kind of challenge*): That's for me to know and you to find out. (39)

This last line is one of the most important in the play because it prepares for the discussion of the imaginary child motif; it is also proof sufficient to refute a whole host of critics who have criticized the ending of the play as a *deus ex machina* effect.

Also important in the talk between George and Nick in this scene is the delineation of the conflict between the two cultures that George (representing history) and Nick (representing biology) epitomize (37, 40). The conflict between these two cultures heightens the personal or sexual conflict of male against male that we see between George and Nick, and it also serves as a springboard to their discussion of Martha's tyrannical father. Here, too, for the first time, we discover the name of the town—New Carthage (40).

When George learns of Nick's intention of settling down and having children, he makes a wide sweeping gesture to include the whole New England countryside and asks, "This is your heart's content—Illyria . . . Penguin Island . . . Gomorrah. . . . You think you're going to be happy here in New Carthage, eh?" (40). These allusions are appropriate to the tone: Illyria, the idyllic seacoast setting of Shakespeare's *Twelfth Night; Penguin Island,* the title and location of Anatole France's novel about illusion and reality; Gomorrah, the wicked city in the Bible where Lot's wife was turned to a pillar of salt; Carthage (ironically) the scene of one of the greatest love stories in all history, that of Dido and Aeneas.

When Honey comes downstairs, at the start of the fourth scene, she tells George that Martha is changing her dress. "Why?" he asks suspiciously. "Why, I imagine she wants to be . . . comfortable," answers Honey. And then she lets the cat out of the bag by saying, "I didn't know until just a minute ago that you had a son."

> GEORGE (*Wheeling, as if struck from behind*): WHAT?
> HONEY: A son! I hadn't known.
> NICK: You to know and me to find out [echoing George]. Well, he must be quite big. . . .
> HONEY: Twenty-one . . . twenty-one tomorrow . . . tomorrow's his birthday.
> NICK (*A victorious smile*) Well!
> GEORGE (*To Honey*): She told you about him? (44)

George repeats this query incredulously two times as if wanting to make absolutely sure of the fact. "*Nailing it down,*" is the way Albee puts it in the stage acting directions (45).

When Nick and Honey offer to leave, George delays their departure: "Oh no, now . . . you mustn't. Martha is changing . . . and Martha is not changing for *me*. Martha hasn't changed for *me* in years. If Martha is changing it means we'll be here for . . . days. You are being accorded an honor, and you must not forget that Martha is the daughter of our beloved boss. She is his . . . right ball, you might say" (47).

Nick objects to George's language in front of Honey. At this point Martha comes in, looking "*more comfortable and . . . this is most important . . . most voluptuous* (47). "Why, Martha," George exclaims, "your Sunday chapel dress!" Martha shows off her dress and immediately begins playing up to Nick and disparaging her husband, an action which constitutes the principal function of this scene. The flattery of Nick takes the form of stressing the early age at which he had received his master's degree (which she had discovered in her upstairs conversation with Honey) and of calling particular attention to his outstanding abilities as a quarterback and an "intercollegiate state middleweight champion" boxer (52).

Martha develops this admiration of athleticism into the same kind of shameless worship of the male body beautiful satirized in *The American Dream*. With remarks like "You look like you still got a pretty good body, *now*" and "you never know when it's going to come in handy," she slowly tortures George. And when Nick says, "I was going to say . . . why give it up until you have to," she concludes "I couldn't agree with you more." Then she repeats this line, and Albee tells us in the stage directions that "*They both smile, and there is a rapport of some unformed sort established*" (52–53). This rapport provides the foundation for her later attempt to seduce Nick.

After George's departure—he anticipates his wife's story—Martha tells of how twenty years ago, her father, having attempted a physical fitness program for his faculty, had played out the example by asking George to put on the gloves with him. George had refused, but Martha had sneaked up behind him and yelled at him. When he turned suddenly around, she had swung at him and knocked him into the huckleberry bushes. "It was awful, really," she explains. "It was funny, but it was awful. . . . I think it's colored our whole life. Really I do! It's an excuse, anyway. . . . It's what he uses for being bogged down, anyway . . . why he hasn't *gone* anywhere" (57).

At this point George reappears, marking the opening of the seventh scene. Behind his back he carries a "short-barreled shotgun," which he suddenly aims "*calmly . . . at the back of* MARTHA's *head.*" As Honey screams, Nick starts up, and Martha turns to face George; he pulls the trigger and says "POW!!!" The stage directions then read: "(*Pop! From the barrel of the gun blossoms out a large red and yellow Chinese parasol.* HONEY *screams again, this time less and mostly from relief.*)" George says to Martha, "You're dead! Pow! You're dead!" And everybody laughs, Honey "*beside herself,*" and Martha almost breaking down, "*her great laugh booming,*" and obviously greatly pleased (57).

The laughter functions as relief from a very tense moment in the complication. What we see in these two scenes is a climactic rendering of the battle of the sexes—first, in the form of actual physical violence—the account of a boxing match between Martha and George which she wins; and, second, in the symbolic murder (a clear victory for him), which marks the seeming culmination of their "war." I say "seeming," because this scene also prepares for a later "murder" of even greater destructive significance to George and Martha. (In this same scene, George says he might kill her some day [60].)

Martha is so pleased by this trick of George's that she asks him to kiss her. When, after some hesitation (because of the company) he finally does, she puts his hand on her breast and wants to go on to an even warmer level of sexual activity, which he refuses to do because of the guests. She grows angry and calls him a "prick." Albee then writes into the text: "GEORGE (*A Pyrrhic* [pun?] *victory*): Everything in its place, Martha . . . everything in its own good time" (59). There may or may not be sexual (or other) symbolism in the way George shows Nick how to put the parasol back in the gun (as though it were being charged for a second, later shot) immediately following this speech.

At any rate, after the guests have been supplied with another round of drinks, Nick moves toward the men's room as Honey calls after him not to bring "any guns, or anything" back with him. Martha then intrudes into this conversation with

> You don't need any props, do you baby?
> NICK: Unh-unh.
> MARTHA (*Suggestive*): I'll bet not. No fake Jap gun for you, eh?
> NICK (*Smiles at* MARTHA.) (61)

The suggestion clearly implies her feeling that George is sexually impotent in comparison to the younger Nick, and the gun here clearly symbolizes the male sexual organ.

In the eighth scene Martha learns that Nick is in the biology department rather than in the mathematics department, as she had previously thought. Her reaction to this information indicates she is still considering Nick as an object of sexual desire:

> So? He's a biologist. Good for him. Biology's even better. It's less . . . abstruse.
>
> (NICK *re-enters*)
>
> You're right at the meat of things, baby. (63)

The ninth scene has two parts. In the first, the quarrel between the sciences and the humanities, begun in the third scene, is developed à la Aldous Huxley's *Brave New World* with Nick himself as a kind of prototype of it[2] (63–69). In the second, the subject of George and Martha's son, introduced in the fourth scene, is renewed (69–75). When Honey asks when their son is coming home, her question leads to discussion of his birthday on the next day, to questions of George's paternity (71), and consequently to questions about the color of the son's eyes.

In George's absence (scene ten), Martha fills in the guests (and the audience) on how she had come to marry George, including her premarital affair during her sophomore year with a gardener's boy at Miss Muff's Academy for Young Ladies, an affair she refers to as "a kind of junior Lady Chatterley arrangement" (78). The marriage plans with George originally had included the prospect of George's succeeding Martha's father in the presidency.

Martha's story spills over into scene eleven, which begins when George returns with the "hooch" (80). At first George goes along cheerfully with Martha's story, because he thinks she is telling about their courtship. But, when he discovers that she is revealing the failure of his hopes and ambitions, after already having divulged the secret about their imaginary son, he warns her that he is becoming very angry. She persists in the tale, however, needling George as she tells how her father seemed to think the succession idea pretty good at first:

> Until he watched for a couple of years! (*To* GEORGE *again*) You getting angrier? (*Now back*) Until he watched for a couple of years and started thinking maybe it wasn't such a good idea after all . . . that maybe Georgie-boy didn't have the *stuff* . . . that he didn't have it in him!
>
> GEORGE (*Still with his back to them all*): Stop it, Martha.
>
> MARTHA (*Viciously triumphant*): The hell I will! You see, George didn't have much push . . . he wasn't particularly . . . aggressive. In fact he was sort of a. . . . (*Spits the word at* GEORGE'S back) . . . A FLOP! A great . . . big . . . fat . . . FLOP! (84)

Simultaneously with this last word, George crashes a bottle against the portable bar and, "*almost crying*," begs Martha not to continue. But she does, needling him about his low salary as an associate professor, his failure to be the kind of person her father and the board of trustees were looking for, and his not being somebody of whom she could be proud. Her voice rises to a feverish climax as he tries to drown her out with the song, "Who's Afraid of Virginia Woolf?"—an alcoholic parody of "Who's Afraid of the Big Bad Wolf," which obliquely fuses antifeminism with nameless fears.

And with this raucous duet, which drunken Honey joins George in singing, against Martha's vituperation, Act I crashes toward a close. Honey becomes sick and retreats down the hall; Nick and Martha follow her. George stands alone, in scene twelve, a completely tragic figure at the curtain. It is impossible for the audience not to pity him, for he is a sympathetic character; and he appears completely defeated.

Since the title of Act I is "Fun and Games," a good question at this point might be: What, specifically, are the *games* Martha and George, as well as their guests, play? A complete list of the games in Act I includes at least the following:

1. The initial quarrel, which George later explains to Nick by saying "Martha and I are merely . . . exercising" (33).
2. George's manipulating the entry of Honey and Nick (he opens the door at the precise moment Martha shouts a vulgar term [19]).
3. George's baiting of Nick, who finally responds in anger —"All right . . . what do you want me to say? Do you want me to say it's funny, so that you can contradict me and say it's sad? or do you want me to say it's sad so you can turn around and say no, it's funny. You can play that damn little game any way you want to, you know!" (33).
4. George's statement to the effect that "Musical beds is the faculty sport around here" (34).
5. The references to other sports—handball (35), football, and boxing (51–52).
6. George's trick with the shotgun and the Chinese parasol (57).
7. Martha's attempt to have George make sexual love to her in front of Honey and Nick and his allusion to this demonstration as "blue games for the guests" (59).
8. Nick's entrance into the spirit of the games by referring to himself as "the wave of the future" and "a personal screwing machine" (68–69).
9. Martha's change of clothes and deliberate play for Nick.
10. Martha's revelation to Honey of the secret son; also, her narrative to the guests about George's failure.

All of these games, in terms of Albee's purpose, relate directly or indirectly to George and Martha's attempts to hurt each other;[3] moreover, they reveal the marital situation of the couple. The episodes in act one follow roughly the order of increasing amounts of pain resulting from this sophisticated kind of play, and the use of the word "fun" to describe the attendant emotional effect on each of the principal participants can only be ironic, for the "fun" hurts. George is hurt most, as the battle stands at the end of act one; and Martha is momentarily triumphant.

Consequently, there can be no mistaking the kind of dramatic representation that *Virginia Woolf* is. It is *serious,* and its distinctive emotional effect, we can already begin to observe, has something to do with the arousal of *pity* and *fear.* We are therefore dealing with *tragedy.*[4] Despite the fact that the language is fierce and in some respects shameless, it is nonetheless appropriate to the struggle for power and survival that is taking place.

If, as we contend, this play really is a tragedy, then the problem of stating the protagonist and the antagonist must be faced. At the end of Act I there can be little doubt that the struggle is between George and Martha and that Martha temporarily has all but vanquished her opponent. As presented in this act, George is the more sympathetic character and therefore our candidate for protagonist; and Martha is his antagonist—at this point in the play!

Obviously the most sensitive character of the play, as developed in this act, George has not yet exhausted his potentialities. His defeat, we repeat, is only temporary. If, as we assume, Albee's purpose is to bring him and Martha together again at the final curtain, something must happen in acts two and three to renew Martha's respect for him; for she cannot love him if she does not respect him. So the stage, in a certain sense, is now set for an exhibition of his intellectual power. He must make a comeback after having drunk the bitter dregs of utter defeat and hopelessness, and he must win the struggle by the use of his wits.

Nevertheless, before this victory can happen—as it does in Act III—Albee shows his virtuosity as a writer by a surprising new development in Act II—a further descent into the inferno of emotional torture for George. This second act is aptly titled *Walpurgisnacht,* for according to the old German legend, on the eve of May Day the witches held an orgiastic sabbath on the heights of the Brocken, the highest peak in the Harz Mountains. Act II continues the development of Act I by showing George's sensibilities—his sense of frustration and defeat—stretched to the snapping point. It is as though Albee were straining the capacities of his character: Just how much of Martha's teasing agony George can endure before making an irrevocable break with her is the general question basic to the action. Or rather, since he is the kind of spirited character who rises to the challenge of her daring games, what means will he take to counterpoise the dreadful power she has to hurt him? And might he not go too far in such an action, causing her to hate him forever? Questions such as these make the play suspenseful and highly interesting from this point to its conclusion.

II *More Talk between George and Nick*

At the beginning of Act II, Nick comes in to tell George that Honey is all right. "Where's my little yum yum? Where's Martha?" asks George. Nick answers, "She's making coffee . . . in the kitchen. She . . . gets sick quite easily" (89). Since both men are preoccupied with their wives, the conversation immediately begins with confusion as to which wife is being mentioned whenever the other refers to "she." And this confusion then develops into antagonism and open threats between Nick and George. But this hostility changes when Nick admits that while flagellation is not his idea of a good time, he yet must admire the efficiency and zeal with which George and Martha pummel each other. "You two are pretty good," he says. "Impressive" (92). Remembering that both men are well intoxicated and that under such circumstances moods can change rather suddenly, we can understand a rather quick switch from hostility to friendliness when George and Nick proceed to exchange confidences.

The confidential talk begins with Nick's explanation as to how Honey tricked him into marrying her because she thought she was pregnant, it having turned out later that she was not. "It was a hysterical pregnancy," he says. "She blew up and then she went down" (94). George then tells Nick about the grandest day of his youth; while in prep school, he had gone on a drinking party with a group of boys, including a particular one who had caused laughter by ordering "bergin and water" and who had accidentally shot his mother.

When Nick asks what happened to the boy later, George tells him that the boy had killed his father, again accidentally, while learning to drive the car. "He swerved the car, to avoid a porcupine, and drove straight into a large tree" (96). This accident had thrown the boy into such a paroxysm of uncontrollable laughter that he had had to be put away in an asylum. "That was thirty years ago," George says. "Is he . . . still there?" asks Nick. George: "Oh, yes. And I'm told that for these thirty years he has . . . not . . . uttered . . . one . . . sound" (96). Following this speech, the stage directions call for *"a rather long silence; five seconds, please"* (96). On stage this is a long and weighty pause, and it heavily underscores the tragedy of George's story.

Abruptly thereafter George shouts twice for Martha, who does not answer. After Nick reminds him that she is in the kitchen making coffee for Honey, the talk turns to what George calls "one of the saddest things," the way men age and the differences between the aging of normal and insane people. According to George, the insane undergo little change, maintaining a "firm-skinned serenity" that leaves them "quite whole" (97). (This talk of aging has been well prepared for in earlier references to differences between George and Nick's ages.)

Sex being seldom long absent from their thoughts, the men discuss again the question of hysterical pregnancies and just plain pregnancies, neither of which Martha has ever had, according to George. When Nick asks about other children besides their son, George says they have only the one son, who is a "comfort, a bean bag" (98). Nick doesn't understand, but Albee is apparently continuing his motif of fun and games: the son, after all, being imaginary, can only be a kind of game (one which George and Martha formerly played only very privately). Consequently, the bean bag, such as small children sometimes play with, is as appropriate an image as any other to represent the son.[5]

George continues his advice to Nick about "accommodation, malleability, adjustment" which he sees as "in the order of things"—the mess of his life, which he has for years been trying to clean up (101–2), contrasts with the mess made by the broken bottle, which he has made no effort to clean up. They also discuss widespread alcoholism in various sections of America—the East and the Midwest, particularly (106). In the talk that follows, Nick admits that he married Honey for her money, thus confirming George's earlier suspicions (102–3); and both men tell of how their fathers-in-law latched onto money crookedly—

the one by robbing the church; the other, the college (107–9).

Their confidential interchanges having progressed this far, Nick now tells George his plan to establish himself in New Carthage by taking over a few courses from the older men, by starting some of his own special groups, and by plowing "a few pertinent wives," including Martha as "the biggest goose in the gangle" (112, 114).

> NICK: Well now, I'd just better get her off in a corner and mount her like a goddam dog, eh?
> GEORGE: Why, you'd certainly better.
> NICK (*Looks at George a minute, his expression a little sick*): You know, I almost think you're serious.
> GEORGE (*Toasting him*): No, baby . . . you almost think you're serious, and it scares the hell out of you. (114)

When George once again tries to give Nick some fatherly advice —"There's quicksand here, and you'll be dragged down, just as [I was] . . ." (115)—Nick refuses to listen to him, laughs at him, and retorts savagely, "UP YOURS!" (116). George then makes one of his longest speeches in the play:

> You take the trouble to construct a civilization . . . to . . . build a society, based on the principles of . . . of principle . . . you endeavor to make communicable sense out of natural order, morality out of the unnatural disorder of man's mind . . . you make government and art, and realize that they are, must be, both the same . . . you bring things to the saddest of all points . . . to the point where there *is* something to lose . . . then all at once, through all the music, through all the sensible sounds of men building, attempting, comes the *Dies Irae*. And what is it? What does the trumpet sound? Up yours! I suppose there's justice to it, after all the years. . . . Up yours. (117)

The absurdity of this speech marks a fitting prelude to the immediate and dramatic appearance of Martha (with Honey) at the beginning of the second scene; for Martha has been the object of their conversation and of Nick's plan. Talk must now yield to action.

III *Two New Games*

Scene two, which continues the fun-and-games motif of Act I, is even longer (117–48) than the first long scene (89–117); it is organized around three games, none of which could be called "funny" except in the most ironic sense—Humiliate the Host, Get the Guests, and Hump the Hostess. Two of these games are played out, and the third is postponed. The first game is preceded by a rather lengthy preface which we must briefly consider in order to understand and appreciate Albee's method.

Shortly after coming on the stage, Martha asks George to apologize for making Honey sick. "I did not make her throw up," retorts George. They argue over the cause of Honey's nausea; and Honey, attempting to quiet their argument, says that she throws up all by herself "without any reason," has, in fact, always done it. "Like Big Ben," remarks George (119). Nick warns George, but Honey babbles on about her curious talent for upchucking (to use Albee's phrase for it), and lets out that before she was married "everybody *thought* it was appendicitis ... but it turned out to be ... it was a ... (*laughs briefly*) ... a false alarm" (119). George and Nick exchange glances at this point, in view of their previous discussion about Honey's having tricked Nick into marriage by her hysterical pregnancy. Martha covers up for Honey by asking George to get her (Martha) a drink and by saying that "George makes everybody sick.... When our son was just a little boy, he used to ... throw up all the time, because of George" (120). George counters that what really made the boy sick was Martha's trying to carry on incest with him.

When Honey thinks she would like a little brandy to "steady" herself, George makes fun of this obvious absurdity: "Hell, you can't walk steady on half a bottle ... got to do it right"; but he adds that he himself used to drink brandy. "You used to drink *bergin*, too," says Martha (My italics [123]). By this means Albee lets the audience in on the fact that Martha, too, had heard (probably *before* that particular night) George's affecting story about the boy who accidentally killed his mother and father.

But is this boy *George*? And if not, what is the point of the story? What does Albee intend to communicate to the audience? If he is hinting at a kind of Oedipean or Oresteian quality for George, as the slayer of his parents, then the similarity to the Greek characters lacks force because it is not developed. If, on the other hand, the boy in the story is *not* George, Albee may have included it to develop George's character by showing us a person something like George who was also suffering from a kind of psychological trauma. A third possibility, of course, is that George is so confused about the boundary between illusion and reality that he actually thinks he is this boy when in fact he is not. But this view of George is hardly consistent with his mental keenness.

A fourth possibility, one which appeals to me most, is that the story about the boy may be like the later business about the novel and the imaginary son—in short, simply one more variety of "fun and games," of self-induced and self-consciously held illusions through which the characters project indications of their psychological states. Whichever of these possible interpretations we decide is the correct one, the play suffers in this instance from lack of clarity.

In response to Martha's query as to what the two men did while the women were in the kitchen, George replies that they "sort of danced around" (123). The conversation then turns to dancing, and this kind of associational rather than logical transition from one thing to the other is characteristic of the way Albee can, in the seemingly static situation of the play, introduce considerable variety and movement. But even before they take up the actual dancing, Martha announces the subject matter of what eventually becomes the first game—George's book. "He didn't run on about how he tried to publish a goddam book, and Daddy wouldn't let him?" she asks Nick. George pleads with Martha not to continue talk of the book as she explains to Nick that he "didn't get the whole sad story" from her husband. Then, tauntingly, she says, "What's the matter with you George? You given up?"

GEORGE (*Calm . . . serious*): No . . . no. It's just I've got to figure out some new way to fight you, Martha. Guerilla tactics, maybe . . . internal subversion . . . I don't know. Something.

MARTHA: Well, you figure it out, and you let me know when you do.

GEORGE (*Cheery*): All right, Love.

HONEY: Why don't we dance? I'd love some dancing. (125)

The dancing, coming as it does between the announcement of the game about George's book and the actual development of it, lends suspense. Furthermore, Honey insists on dancing alone like a ballerina and becomes angry with Nick when he stops her. Then Martha pairs off with Nick and dances seductively with him as she tells him about George's novel containing, apparently, the same story George had earlier told Nick of how the boy had contributed, however accidentally, to the deaths of his mother and father.

Martha also tells Nick how her father threatened to fire George if he published this novel, and how George had told him that it wasn't a novel at all, but the *truth*. Unable to restrain himself, George rushes Martha and attempts to strangle her. Nick grabs him and throws him on the floor, while Honey excitedly shouts "VIOLENCE! VIOLENCE!" as she enjoys the sight of the struggling figures (137–38). Gradually they regain their composure as George says,

> Well! That's one game. What shall we do now, hunh? (MARTHA *and* NICK *laugh nervously*) Oh come on . . . let's think of something else. We've played Humiliate the Host . . . we've gone through that one . . . What shall we do now? . . . Let's see now . . . what else can we do? There are other games. How about . . . Hump the Hostess? . . . Or is that for later . . . mount her like a goddam dog? . . . You don't wanna play that now, hunh? You wanna save that game till later? Well, what'll we play now? We gotta play a game.
>
> MARTHA (*Quietly*): Portrait of a man drowning.
>
> GEORGE (*Affirmatively, but to none of them*): I am not drowning. . . . I've got it! I'll tell you what game we'll play. We're done with that . . . and we don't want to play Hump the Hostess, yet . . . not yet . . . So I know what we'll play. . . . We'll play a round of Get the Guests. How about that? How about a little game of Get the Guests? (138–40)

George then proceeds to relate in the form of a veiled allegory with a gradual disclosure the story that Nick had told him earlier—of how Honey's father had robbed the church and how Nick had married Honey for money. At the climax of this emergence of the skeleton from the Nick and Honey closet, Honey realizes that Nick has told George the greatest secret of their private life, and she runs hysterically from the room, crying to her husband, "Leave me alone . . . I'm going . . . to . . . be . . . sick" (148). The mental agony George endured in the first game is balanced, therefore, by what Honey and Nick go through in this second one.

In scene three, which is short (148–50), Nick threatens George with violence for disturbing Honey, and Martha tells him to go look after his wife. While he is off-stage seeing about her, George and Martha have a quiet conversation (scene four) during which Martha explains to him that their relationship has snapped. Twenty-three years of marriage have come to naught, she explains to him:

MARTHA: . . . I sat there at Daddy's party, and I watched you . . . I watched you sitting there, and I watched the younger men around you, the men who were going somewhere. And I sat there and I watched you, and *you* weren't *there!* And it snapped! It finally snapped! And I'm going to howl it out, and I'm not going to give a damn what I do, and I'm going to make the damnest biggest explosion you ever heard.
GEORGE (*Very pointedly*): You try and I'll beat you at your own game.
MARTHA (*Hopefully*): Is that a threat, George? Hunh? (158)

IV *The Third Game*

The remaining six scenes of this act (159–81, scenes five through ten) are unified with the playing out of the third game, Hump the Hostess, one well-prepared for by scenes one, two, and four. With Honey recuperating comfortably on the tiles of the bathroom floor (160) and with George sent for ice for her, Martha and Nick are free to continue their sex play. When George returns and sees what they are doing (165), he refuses to give them the satisfaction of noticing them; instead, he pretends to curl up contentedly with a book. His doing so makes Martha furious, "*livid*" in fact (171), since she obviously is using Nick to make George jealous.

The book George reads is Spengler's *Decline of the West*, and the passage Albee has chosen from it as appropriate to the marital situation in the play is read aloud by George not only for the audience's benefit but also as though he were pondering it: "And the West, encumbered by crippling alliances, and burdened with a morality too rigid to accommodate itself to the swing of events, must . . . eventually . . . fall" (174). In a fury, he throws the book at the door chimes, which "*crash against one another, ringing wildly.*" The effect dramatizes his feeling toward Martha, now in the kitchen alone with Nick.

Honey, who had fallen asleep on the bathroom floor—sucking her thumb, according to George (167)—but who is now awakened by the noise of the chimes, tells George her dream. In the process of relating it, she also reveals her hitherto well-guarded secret—she does not want children, is afraid of having them; in fact, her headaches and nausea stem from the pills she takes to prevent childbirth (176). When, from off-stage, Martha's laughter is heard amid a crash of dishes, George tries to explain to Honey what is happening in the kitchen; but she says she doesn't understand him and asks who rang the doorbell.

This query sets George thinking. He conceives his trump trick against Martha: the idea of a messenger's having come to announce the death of their son. Martha's laugh again is heard off-stage, Honey says she is sick and thinks she is going to die; but George practices his announcement *"very softly, so* MARTHA *could not possibly hear him"*: "Martha? Martha? I have some . . . terrible news for you. (*There is a strange half-smile on his lips*) It's about our . . . son. He's dead. Can you hear me, Martha? Our boy is dead. (*He begins to laugh, very softly . . . it is mixed with crying*) CURTAIN" (181).

In analyzing this effect, we note that, as usual, the imaginary son is a symbol. The fact that George regards him as dead at the moment he thinks Martha is either copulating, or near to copulating, with Nick means simply that the son is a symbol of George and Martha's relationship. With the death of this relationship seemingly imminent, it is also appropriate that the son should die. And for this reason George's semi-hysterical mixture of soft laughter and tears at the curtain is perfectly appropriate. His tears show that he cares, and deeply, for Martha. A tragic, defeated, and pitiable character at the end of act one, he is much more so at the end of act two; for he thinks he has lost the thing that defines him—his relationship to Martha.

The third and last act provides a semi-happy turn of events to George's *Walpurgisnacht,* his descent into the underworld, or whatever we may wish to call it. Copulation is not necessarily the same thing as love, and there is such a thing as sexual impotence under the extreme influence of alcohol. Put to the test, Nick, it seems, could not make love to Martha. But everything does not automatically turn out for the best. There are still matters of probability to be considered.

One set of probabilities, in Act II, calls for a sexual action of some sort between Nick and Martha. But Albee has been careful, too, to insert throughout both Act I and II another set of probabilities. These concern the basic fact that both George and Martha really care very much, and very deeply about, if not for, each other. But, because of the rules of the various games they play and because of their spirited and intellectually discriminating natures, it rarely is in good taste for them to admit this fact, either to themselves or to anyone else. The dramatist has the problem, therefore, of constructing a resolution that will take into account both sets of probabilities. Nick's failure to perform the sex act solves the problem and permits Albee in the third act, as we shall see, to bring together George and Martha at the final curtain.

V *Exorcism*

Act III, entitled "The Exorcism," obviously refers to the casting out of devils encountered in the *Walpurgisnacht* of Act II. Indeed, what other defense can one make of any debauchery or orgy? Even the Dionysian revels were religious ceremonies. We are prepared, therefore, for a change, or turn, in the drama at the beginning of this act. Aristotle's contention that Greek tragedy usually had such a turn, which divided it into the two parts of *complication* and *denouement*, applies to the two-part play Albee has written: Acts I and II follow a continuous line of developmental torture for George, while Act III frees him, at least partially, by exorcism of the devils that torture him.[6]

By "devils" I don't mean Martha and Nick, but the subconscious forces—jealousy, pride, anger, hatred, bestiality, frustration, defeat, and despair—to which married people who must repress these emotions behind a brave front of everything-is-all-right-because-we-love-each-other are certainly no strangers. In this play the well-layered skin is ripped asunder, the bones are cracked, and the very marrow penetrated (212–13). But the final effect of this searching dissection is not only to exorcise these devils from George (and Martha—to a lesser extent, even from Nick and Honey) but also to purge the audience of feelings of pity and fear felt for George (and to some degree even for Martha). Thus the exorcism operates on two levels.[7]

Act III, the shortest in the play (185–242), contains six scenes. Or, to use our more basic rationale of the games—for these constitute the real backbone of the play and are ordered roughly according to increasing dramatic intensity—we might say that the final act presents two more games—Houseboy and Bringing up Baby. The first scene presents Martha alone, talking to herself; and the most important part of her long soliloquy shows her wishfully thinking about making up with George: "Can I get you a drink, Martha? Why, thank you, George; that's very kind of you. No, Martha, no; why I'd do anything for you. Would you, George? Why, I'd do anything for you, too. Would you, Martha? Why, certainly, George. Martha, I've misjudged you. And I've misjudged you, too, George" (185).

Her mood has clearly changed; and, furthermore, it changes rhapsodically in the course of the soliloquy. At one point she lapses into a lachrymose vein, imagining she is addressing her father: "I cry all the time too, Daddy. I cry alllll *[sic]* the time; but deep inside, so no one can see me. I cry all the time. And Georgie cries all the time, too. We both cry all the time, and then, what we do, we cry, and we take our tears, and we put 'em in the ice box, in the goddamn ice trays... until they're frozen ... and then ... we put them ... in our ... drinks" (185–86). But her tearful mood is interspersed with laughter; and, when Nick comes in and says they are all crazy, she replies: "Awww, 'tis the refuge we take when the unreality of the world weighs too heavy on our tiny heads" (187–88).

Scene two informs the audience of Nick's failure to achieve sexual union with Martha. We learn, moreover, that George after all is the sole man in Martha's life who has ever made her happy. As she phrases it, it is "... George who is out somewhere there in the dark.... George who is good to me, and whom I revile; who understands me, and whom I push off; who can make me laugh, and I choke it back in my throat; who can hold me, at night, so that it's warm, and whom I will bite so there's blood; who keeps learning the games we play as quickly as I can change the rules; who can make me happy and I do not wish to be happy, and yes I do wish to be happy. George and Martha: sad, sad, sad" (190–91).

It is George, she continues, who "has made the hideous, the hurting, the insulting mistake of loving me and must be punished for it . . . who tolerates, which is intolerable; who is kind, which is cruel; who understands, which is beyond comprehension . . ." (191). Thus the probability for their reunion is set up. Also, in this conversation with Nick she defends George despite Nick's criticism of him as a person lacking backbone (191–92). And, finally, when the door chimes ring, she peremptorily orders Nick to answer the door.

When he fails to understand, she shouts at him, "Answer it! . . . You can be houseboy around here for a while. You can start off being houseboy right now." When Nick remonstrates that he is "no flunky" to her, she replies cheerfully, "Sure you are! You're ambitious, aren't you, boy? You didn't chase me around the kitchen and up the goddam stairs out of mad, driven passion, did you now? You were thinking a little bit about your career, weren't you? Well, you can just houseboy your way up the ladder for a while" (194). She adds insult to injury by singing "Just a gigolo" as Nick goes to answer the door.

As Nick flings open the door, ushering in scene three—this business balances the earlier scene in Act I where George flings the door open for the arrival of Nick and Honey—a great bunch of snapdragons is thrust in and a voice *"in a hideously cracked falsetto"* intones the well-known refrain from Tennessee Williams' *A Streetcar Named Desire*: "Flores; flores para los muertos. Flores" (195). Martha recognizes George in this amusing stage business, even before he becomes visible by stepping into the room, and she laughs.

The effect of his entrance is truly grotesque, for the audience knows that, behind this practical joke, George is really intent on announcing the death of their son. George carries the joke yet further by pretending to mistake Nick for the imaginary son. "Sonny!" exclaims George, attempting to embrace him, "You've come home for your birthday!" Nick shies away from George's outstretched arms, and Martha exclaims "Ha, ha, ha, HA! That's the houseboy, for God's sake" (196). The flowers include pansies, rosemary, and violets—all of which were in Martha's wedding bouquet. (Intoxicated, she mispronounces *violets* as "violence" [196], but her mistake is tonally right for the game they are about to play.)

Nick begins to think about leaving, but George says they have one more game to play besides that of houseboy. Martha had at first told George that Nick could not function sexually in the kitchen, but later she had lied to him that Nick "had made it in the sack" (202). Feeling that he has been cuckolded, George now retreats into a mood of quiet vindictiveness by throwing the snapdragons one at a time at Martha and Nick as though they were small spears; and he times his throws to punctuate his caustic remarks. There yet remains one game to play, says George; and noticing Honey's absence, he bellows out a hog call for her. Nick goes to fetch her from the bathroom. George wants everyone present for this final game.

In a melting mood, Martha pleads for no more games (206–9), but George insists. In fact, he deliberately maddens her for this particular bout, saying, "I want you on your feet and slugging, sweetheart, because I'm going to knock you around, and I want you up for it." As she becomes angry and begins shouting again, he says, "Good for you, girl; now, we're going to play this one to the death" (209).

Nick returns with Honey and the fifth scene—the longest and most important in the act—commences. Albee wrings the maximum emotional effect from this scene by first building up in a *scène-à-faire* technique Martha and George's highly romanticized, and so all the more pathetic, corporate and individual illusions about this nonexistent child (217–24). I call this a *scène-à-faire* because the audience must actually see Martha and George at the work of illusion-building or dreaming in order to be convinced that the imaginary-son business is perhaps the most real thing in their entire marriage.

Albee handles this scene with particular skill. For example, since George and Martha are essentially different personalities, each has a different version of the dream—of such matters as the relative ease of the birth, the color of the eyes, and the like. Yet they must agree, or compromise on these matters, for here, if anywhere, they must show some cooperative spirit; otherwise creation would be impossible:

MARTHA: It was an easy birth. . . .
GEORGE: Oh, Martha; no. You labored . . . how you labored.
MARTHA: It was an easy birth . . . once it had been . . . accepted, relaxed into.
GEORGE: Ah . . . yes. Better. (217)

So carried away is Martha by her creative dreaming of her green-eyed son that she does not even remonstrate when George, definitely for once in the play in an agreeable mood, says the eyes of the child were "blue, green, brown" (220). In a rapture she attains the first climax of her story, talking of the child's love of the sun, his tanned complexion, his fleecy hair—her (she lets herself be corrected to "*our*") "beautiful, beautiful boy" (218, 220).

This little climax attained, she goes on to greater heights. Here, for variety and richness, Albee introduces a duet effect; George murmurs in Latin phrases from the mass while Martha recounts how their son broke his arm at the age of three and how he had come to epitomize, at least for her, truth, beauty, wisdom, and perfection. At this specific point George sympathetically chimes in, "There's a real mother talking" (222). Ironical as his statement is, it suggests the coalescence between truth and illusion that other passages of thought in the play have also hinted at (see 202, for example). Here, too, Honey interrupts "*almost tearfully,*" having decided, as a result of listening to Martha's eloquent speech, that she now really wants a child (222–23).

Following this interruption, which Martha patiently waits out without really paying attention to it, Albee again shows his excellent sense of well-paced timing and variety by reinforcing consistency of characterization. He does so with the following turn:

> MARTHA: . . . Of course, this state, this perfection . . . couldn't last. Not with George . . . not with George around.
>
> GEORGE (*To the others*): There; you see? I knew she'd shift. (223)

The battle, temporarily at a lull, waits to renew itself like a phoenix just before rebirth. A phoenix is always a phoenix; Martha must always be Martha, and George must be George. At least, that is what the audience thinks and expects. But Martha is tired; and having brought her auditors up to the point where the boy is away at college and "everything is fine," she intends to end the narrative there.

George, however, will not let her off so easily; he inflames her with insult. The phoenix is reborn, and the battle fires burn brighter than ever, culminating in a brilliant duet of great emotional intensity which Martha ends with, "I have tried to protect, to raise above the mire of this vile, crushing marriage; the one light in all this hopeless . . . *darkness* . . . our SON," while George intones in Latin that part of the mass dealing with the day of judgment (227). Honey begs him to stop and Nick asks, "Is this game over?" (228).

"Ho-ho! Not by a long shot," responds George. Then he turns to Martha and says, "We got a little surprise for you, baby. It's about sunny-Jim," (228). And he tells her of the death of their son:

> GEORGE: Martha . . . (*Long pause*) . . . our son is . .. dead. (*Silence*) He was . . . killed . . . late in the afternoon. . . . (*Silence*) (*A tiny chuckle*) on a country road, with his learner's permit in his pocket, he swerved, to avoid a porcupine, and drove straight into a. . . .
> MARTHA (*Rigid fury*): YOU . . . CAN'T . . . DO . . . THAT!
> GEORGE: . . . large tree. (231)

After repeated insistence that George cannot decide such matters independently of her and after trying to attack him in a wild rage and having her arms pinioned from behind by Nick (who tries to control her), she at last listens to what George is saying: "Now listen, Martha; listen carefully. We got a telegram; there was a car accident, and he's dead. Pouf! Just like that! Now, how do you like it?" (233). Her answer is a *"howl which weakens into a moan"*—*"N O O O O O O o o o o o o"* (233).

This most powerful emotional effect in the entire play is a real *discovery* in the Aristotelian sense—similar to that tragic and awful moment of Sophocles' *Oedipus,* when Oedipus discovers he has not only unwittingly killed his own father but has also married his own mother and fathered her children.[8] When he reports that there had been a telegram, but that he had eaten it, she spits in his face. She realizes, of course, that George has killed the imaginary child deliberately. When she asks him why, he reminds her of the rules and tells her she had broken them by mentioning their son to someone else. Honey confirms this breach of the rules, crying "To me. You mentioned him to me." Martha, crying, defends her breaking of their pact: "I FORGET! Sometimes . . . sometimes when it's night, when it's late, and . . . and everybody else is . . . talking . . . I forget and I . . . want to mention him ... but I ... HOLD ON ... I hold on ... but I've wanted to ... so often ... oh, George, you've *pushed* it ... there was no need ... there was no need for *this.* I *men*tioned him ... all right ... but you didn't have to push it over the EDGE. You didn't have to ... kill him" (237).

George's only reply is the benediction of the mass, after which he says "It will be dawn soon. I think the party's over" (237). In response to Nick's query about children, Martha and George, speaking together and with "*a hint of communion,*" admit that they could not have any.

Even after Nick and Honey have gone, in the sixth and last scene Martha still asks George, "Did you ... did you ... have to?" (239). He says he did, that it was time, implying that they had played this particular game of the imaginary child too long, that their life would now be better. But, after a long silence, neither of them is sure of this particular point. "Just ... us?" asks Martha, to which George replies, "Yes."

> MARTHA: I don't suppose, maybe, we could. . . .
> GEORGE: No, Martha. (241)

We cannot be certain exactly what is intended here, but the probability seems to be that Martha is suggesting some new escape game. And this interpretation makes the play a *tragedy,* for the dramatist seems to imply that George and Martha were probably happier while under the influence of the illusion. Divesting themselves of the illusion has brought them nearer to reality, but the attendant loss has also brought about their fall by introducing them to an even deeper sorrow than anything yet experienced in their lives. Consequently, we pity them. He asks her if she is all right, and her answer is an ambiguous "Yes. No" (241). As he puts his hand gently on her shoulder and sings softly to her the repetitious phrases of "Who's Afraid of Virginia Woolf?" she answers, and repeats, "I ... am ... George ..." (241–42). On this note, with a tableau, the play comes to a close.

Albee has succeeded in persuading us that Martha, as well as George, is a genuinely pitiable character. Thus one can say that the plot contains a kind of reversal; for while Martha had the upper hand over him in her role of his antagonist during the first two acts, he now has won at the fun-and-games business—but at so considerable a cost as to amount to only a pyrrhic victory. At least, however, they communicate, understand each other, and are together at the curtain. They are nevertheless so weakened by the strain of the exorcism and by the bleak prospect that lies before them that we can only pity both of them. It seems to me that we see in them something of the whole general problem of humanity suffering from forces beyond its control, forces which lie inside us as well as outside us and which make us fearful when we recognize them. Martha's fear, then, is exactly the right note for the terminal effect of this highly indeterminate ending.

CHAPTER 8

Adaptations from Novels

ALBEE'S second Broadway play, *The Ballad of the Sad Cafe* (1963), failed to repeat the great success of *Who's Afraid of Virginia Woolf?* One argument adduced for this failure was that he had adapted another author's work—Carson McCullers' novella of the same name (1951).[1] An even greater degree of failure attended his later adaptation of James Purdy's novel *Malcolm* (1966).

I The Ballad of the Sad Cafe

The setting is of unusual importance in the total emotional effect of *The Ballad of the Sad Cafe.* The first stage direction reads: "*Noon sun; street deserted; house boarded up; nothing moves, no one is to be seen; heat; quiet. Music: under all or some of the following*" (3). The time is August, a hot "August afternoon," according to the Narrator's first speech (3). The place, although not specified, is a small town in the South. Miss Amelia's house occupies most of the stage, "*not centered . . . but tending to stage-right, leaving a playing area, stage-left, for the battle which will take place out-of-doors*" (2). Other stage directions specify "*practical*" use of Miss Amelia's house with interior and exterior, upstairs and downstairs all somewhat visible. "*The main street of the town runs before the porch of the house, parallel to the apron of the stage*" (2).

When the Narrator comes on stage, he delineates more details of the setting, pointing out Miss Amelia's "boarded up house" as the oldest and largest building in town. By contrast, the town is "not very old," nor very large. The town has a "cotton mill, the two-room houses where the workers live, a few peach trees, a church with two water-colored windows, and a miserable main street only a hundred yards long." The Narrator describes the town as "lonesome—sad—like a place that is far off and estranged from all other places in the world." On a hot August afternoon "There is nothing whatever to do. . . .There is heat . . . and silence . . ." (3).

The Narrator calls attention to the second-story shuttered window of the house. The shutters open slowly, and we see Miss Amelia for the first time, as the Narrator says: "Sometimes, in the late afternoon, when the heat is at its worst, a hand will slowly open the shutter there, and a face will look down at the town . . . a terrible dim face . . . like the faces known in dreams. The face will linger at the window for an hour or so . . . then the shutters will be closed once more, and as likely as not there will not be another soul to be seen along the main street" (4).

Once, the Narrator goes on, this boarded-up house was a lively cafe: "It was the center of town! And this cafe . . . was run by a Miss Amelia Evans . . . who lives up there even now . . . whose face, in the late afternoon, sometimes when the heat is at its worst, can be seen peering out from that shuttered window," like, we might add, a blasted soul. The Narrator then carries us back in time to an April evening eight years before, when the house was "a general store." As he explains, there are two stories to be told—"how the cafe came into being . . . and how the cafe . . . died. How we came to . . . silence" (4).

Although Albee has indicated that this play is meant to be presented continuously without interruption, and although he says there are two stories, the action obviously falls into five major divisions which bear some resemblance to conventional acts. (For variety of comment and perspective on this action, he provides two choruses—the townsmen and the Narrator.) There are also two long flashbacks, one within the other; but these occur within the frame of the Narrator's story in the present. "The Opening of the Cafe," the first of these divisions (4–38), includes several shorter scenes and covers approximately three days and nights.

The first scene in the larger of the two flashbacks introduces the audience to three townsmen—Stumpy MacPhail and the Rainey twins (Rainey 1 and Rainey 2)—who lounge around the store. A fourth character, Henry Macy, arrives and is queried about how his brother Marvin is "enjoying the penitentiary" (6). All four of these men are waiting to buy liquor from Miss Amelia, who is "at the still" (6).

In scene two Miss Amelia appears, "*carrying several dark glass bottles.*" She is "*dressed in Levis and a cotton work shirt (red?), boots*" (7). Laconic is the word for her; she is there for one, and for only one, purpose—to sell them liquor. When Henry Macy looks far down the road to the left and sees something coming, the men speculate on what it is. "It's a calf got loose," remarks Rainey 1. "No; it's somebody's youngun," say Rainey 2 (10). But the figure is a hunchback dwarf, Cousin Lymon, carrying a battered suitcase and looking for his cousin, Miss Amelia Evans. Cousin Lymon's entry marks the beginning of scene three.

Although he explains his kinship to her in great detail, Miss Amelia is seemingly unmoved by his account until he "*sits down on the steps and suddenly begins to cry*" (13). At this point Miss Amelia takes pity on him, touches the hump on his back, and offers him a free drink from her own private flask. The men pay for their whiskey, and she invites her cousin, Lymon Willis by name, to "come on in" and have the supper left on the stove (15). Then she invites him to stay: "There is a room for you upstairs . . . where you can sleep . . . when you are done eating" (16).

Left alone, in scene three, the three townsmen—Henry Macy had already departed, ostensibly not to have to see Miss Amelia beat up the dwarf (13)—are baffled by her uncustomary treatment of this male. It speedily become apparent that they function as a chorus: "I never seen nothing like that in my life," comments Rainey 1. "What's she up to? Miss Amelia never invite *[sic]* people into her house . . . eat from her table. What she up to?" (17). They guess that she may plan to rob him, thinking there may be "something in that suitcase of his," and then "kill him" (17). A fadeout emphasizes this ominous thought.

When the lights come on, it is morning. In scene four Henry Macy appears. When Amelia asks him if he wants to buy, he says no. Brusquely she tells him the store is "closed"; "I am off to tend to some land I bought . . . up near Fork Falls Road" (19). As other curious townspeople saunter in, the suspicion grows that she has murdered the dwarf for his money and is going away to bury his body in the swamp land "up near Fork Falls Road" (19). (Miss Amelia's penchant for grabbing up land by foreclosing mortgages is mentioned by Emma [20] and is apparently well known to the others.)

The townspeople talk all day about this exciting possibility.

But, as the Narrator explains, in scene five, when it came "evening and Miss Amelia returned from her business, and they saw that there were no bloodstains on her anywhere, the consternation grew" (27). At eight o'clock that night, the townspeople, feeling that the "time beyond which questions may not stay unanswered" (28) has been reached, file into the store to confront her. To their great surprise, they see Cousin Lymon descend the stairs—very much alive but quite changed: "HE *is no longer ragged;* HE *is clean;* HE *wears his little coat, but neat and mended, a red and black checkered shirt, knee breeches, black stockings, shoes laced up over the ankles, and a great lime green shawl, with fringe, which almost touches the ground. The effect is somehow regal . . . or papal. The room is as still as death*" (29).

When Miss Amelia appears (scene six), she asks, "Does anyone want waiting on?" The men buy liquor and drink it right there on the premises. Hitherto, explains the Narrator, the rule had been that "they must drink it outside her premises—and there was no feeling of joy in the transaction" (35). But from this moment on "Miss Amelia broke her rule, and the men could drink in her store. More than that, she furnished glasses and opened two boxes of crackers so that they were there hospitably in a platter on the counter and anyone who wished could take one free. . . . Now, this was the beginning of the cafe" (35).

Miss Amelia surprises everyone by asking Cousin Lymon if he wants his whiskey straight or "warmed in a pan with water on the stove"; he prefers the latter. The townspeople are aghast when Cousin Lymon addresses Miss Amelia familiarly as "Amelia." When Merlie Ryan concludes that Miss Amelia is in love, general rejoicing ensues. The Narrator then relates: "This opening of the cafe came to an end at midnight. Everyone said goodbye to everyone else in a friendly fashion. . . . And so ended three days and nights in which had come the arrival of a stranger, an unholy holiday, and the start of the cafe" (38).

The second act, which takes place four years later, includes a long flashback: "The hunchback continued to live with Miss Amelia. The cafe expanded in a gradual way, and Miss Amelia began to sell her liquor by the drink, and some tables were brought into the store, and there were customers every evening, and on Saturday nights a great crowd. The place was a store no longer but had become a proper cafe, and was open every evening from six until twelve o'clock" (38). By this time Cousin Lymon's presence in Miss Amelia's house had also been accepted—by almost everyone but a few females (38).

At the beginning of this second act, "towards evening" (38), we see Miss Amelia and Cousin Lymon sitting on the steps outside the cafe. She is massaging his shoulders, and we learn that she has given up the idea that he will ever grow up (39).

The function of the first long scene (38-49) is to characterize Cousin Lymon and Miss Amelia and to show the development of their odd relationship: she mothers him, and he makes strange demands upon her. While going through her curio cabinet, he has found an acorn, one she had picked up on the day her father died, and her two kidney stones, souvenirs of her operation. As she reminisces about her father, who was a moonshiner and whom she had loved, the dwarf makes demands. He wants a smaller-sized bed: her father's bed, in which he had been sleeping, is too long. He needs a great gold chain on which to hang her two kidney stones. She may keep the acorn, he says, but he must have the gold chain with her stones. And he asks her to drive him into Cheehaw on Sunday to see the movie show or go to the fair. Moreover, he complains that "The grits we had this morning was poor; fried too quick so that the inside never heated," and he demands that they be "exactly right" (45).

When Miss Amelia indulgently promises him everything he asks, he says he loves her; but he says it "*coldly*" (48). The Narrator comments on this statement by explaining that "there are many kinds of love ... [and that] there was only one part of her life that she did not want Cousin Lymon to share with her ... to know about; and it concerned a man named Marvin Macy" (49).

The second scene (49–63) takes place *inside* the cafe on the same Saturday night. "*Everyone is there*" enjoying the chicken dinner for twenty cents (49). Henry Macy, the brother of Marvin, is drinking but not eating. Under questioning by Miss Amelia as to why he is not *eating* as well as drinking, Henry reveals that he has received a letter from his brother Marvin, recently paroled from the penitentiary. Miss Amelia reacts coldly to this announcement, but Cousin Lymon wants to know all about Marvin. At approximately this same moment Marvin Macy appears outside the cafe; gazing at it, he whittles and whistles softly.

The second long flashback then commences. Covering pages 63–107 and about eleven short scenes, its chief function is to provide information about the earlier marriage of Miss Amelia and Marvin Macy. Besides developing the new character, Marvin Macy, it also sets up the probability for the affectionate regard of Marvin by Cousin Lymon because Marvin appeals to his imagination. The dwarf's cooling toward Miss Amelia also points to this development. Briefly, the flashback is the dramatization of what Cousin Lymon found out from townspeople about Miss Amelia's earlier marriage to Marvin Macy, when Miss Amelia was nineteen years old and when Marvin Macy, ten years younger than his brother Henry and then "a loom-fixer at the mill . . . [,] was the handsomest man in the region . . . and the wildest" (63). From Marvin's conversation with Henry, we learn that Marvin apparently had the habit of taking young girls walking in the woods, of befuddling them with marijuana, and of seducing them.

Scene two shows Marvin's failing to rise when Miss Amelia appears on the scene, her hating him, and his realizing that she is "grown up" (67–72). After he angers her and she goes back inside, he tells his brother that he wants her for his wife (72–74). Scene four (75–83) shows him, after having spent two years in bettering his character, finally proposing to her. He comes courting her in "*his dressy suit*" on Sunday night, carrying "*a sack of chitterlins, a bunch of swamp flowers and . . . a silver ring*" (75). He proposes to her, and she greedily accepts the ring and his promise of ten acres of timber land. But she won't let him kiss her, and she is disappointed to hear that he had not really, as reported, cut off the ear of a man in Cheehaw during a fight (80). According to the Narrator, they were married next Sunday—for "ten unholy days" (83).

The next scene (83–86) shows them alone on their wedding night. She talks about a deal in kindling wood and doesn't understand his intentions when he wants to go to bed. When she comes downstairs one-half hour later, "her face black with anger" (87), she goes to the office and spends the night there, according to the report of Emma Hale, "who had watched it *[this scene]*, her nose pressed against the downstairs window of the store" (86). In scene six Emma Hale tells what she saw to Henry Macy, brother of the groom (86–87).

Marvin tries to woo his wife with wedding gifts (scene seven, 87-89), but she merely sells the presents—"an enamel brooch, an opal ring, and a silver bracelet which had hanging from it two silver lovebirds"—and eats up his offering of a box of chocolates (89). Scene eight shows Marvin nonplussed by her behavior, for he really loves her, he confides to his brother (89–90). Then Marvin, as a last resort, deeds over to her his ten acres of timber land (scene nine, 90–100); but she still refuses to sleep with him. Indeed, when he makes overtures to her, she hits him in the jaw with her fist, breaking one of his teeth, and then threatens him with a shotgun.

In the next-to-last scene (100-4) Henry again appears in his role of confidant to Marvin, who dictates a letter to his wife before leaving forever. The letter shows his mixture of frustration and deep-seated love for her. He threatens to kill her, yet closes, "With all my love very truly yours your husband Marvin Macy." He signs it by pricking his thumb and putting a blood stamp of his thumb on it. Then he says good-by to his brother. After he is gone (scene eleven), Henry tells Miss Amelia; and she says "good riddance" (106–7).

At the end of this extended flashback (within the larger flashback that is almost the entire play), Cousin Lymon taxes Miss Amelia with having kept the secret of her marriage from him (scene three of act two, 107–13). Marvin Macy's life, however, fascinates him—even Marvin's experience as a member of a chain gang—and the dwarf makes the point that these men sing because they are "*together*" (112). Miss Amelia reminds him that she and he are together, but he dismisses this fact, preferring to dwell on the togetherness of the men in the chain gang (112–13).

In the fourth scene (113–16) Marvin Macy appears, as he had before the flashback on the ill-fated marriage; and Miss Amelia tells him to "clear out!" (114). When he sees Cousin Lymon, he calls him a "bug"; but Lymon is excited by Marvin and "*begins small, involuntary spasms of excitement, little jumps from the ground, strange jerks of the hands*" (114). Even after Marvin knocks him down for staring at him, he follows him devotedly off-stage, thus dramatizing his break with Miss Amelia and his doglike affection for Marvin. Miss Amelia now realizes that Cousin Lymon does not love her, and the Narrator launches into a rather long, preachy discussion of love, including the different experiences of the lover and the beloved: "Now, the beloved can also be of any description; the most outlandish people can be the stimulus for love" (116).

The last scene of the act (117–22) presents the Macy brothers and Cousin Lymon, who has been following Marvin for a week:

> MARVIN MACY: You been followin' me around near a week now, wigglin' your ears at me, flappin' around, dancin'. . . you don't go home 'cept for your eats and bed. What you expectin' me to do . . . *adopt* you?
>
> COUSIN LYMON (*With exaggerated longing*): Oh, Marvin Macy . . . would you? Would you do that?
>
> MARVIN MACY (*Takes a swipe at him which* COUSIN LYMAN *ducks expertly, laughs*): Damn little lap dog. (*But there is kindness in the contempt*) (119).

When Henry asks Marvin how long he is staying, Marvin tells him to mind his own business.

To sum up the function of this long complex second act as a whole, we may say that it shows: (1) the development of Miss Amelia's maternal love for Cousin Lymon; (2) Marvin Macy's supplanting her as an object of Cousin Lymon's interest and affection; and (3) the exposition on the earlier unsuccessful marriage and consequent hatred between Marvin and Miss Amelia.

The next division, what I am somewhat arbitrarily calling "act three" (122–33), begins ominously with the Narrator's saying that "it was the beginning of the destruction. And the things that happened next were beyond the imagination" (122). If the function of the first act has been to bring together Cousin Lymon and Miss Amelia and to present the opening of the cafe as a tangible, symbolical expression of Miss Amelia's affection for him, and if the function of the second act has been to present the development of a counterforce or circumstance likely to disturb the progress of this affection (namely Miss Amelia's previous marriage to Marvin Macy, hitherto unknown to Cousin Lymon, including the reappearance of Marvin Macy after his parole from the penitentiary and Lymon's attraction to him), the third act then follows logically by showing the almost complete separation of Lymon from Miss Amelia because of Marvin Macy. Should Marvin be removed, there might yet be time for salvaging something of the earlier emotional relationship existing between Miss

Amelia and Cousin Lymon. The suspenseful question in act three, then, is whether Marvin Macy is just passing through or whether he means to stay as a permanent obstacle to Miss Amelia.

The third act has three scenes. In the first (122–25), "*a usual evening*" in the cafe with most of the townspeople present, Emma Hale notices that Cousin Lymon is conspicuously absent. She says, "It seem strange to have everybody here save one. (*Murderously solicitous*) I mean when poor Cousin Lymon ain't here to join in the merriment, an' have his little supper, an' be such an enter*tain*ment for us all, an' to keep you *company*, Miss Amelia?" (123).

In the next scene (125–27), which brings in Henry Macy, Miss Amelia guardedly asks him if he has seen Cousin Lymon; and he replies that Lymon is with Marvin "again," "not far off . . ." (125). In the third and last scene of this act (127–33), Cousin Lymon appears and announces that he has brought "a special guest for dinner tonight"—Marvin Macy. When Marvin comes in, he orders Lymon, whom he calls "brokeback," to bring his dinner. Amid great tension, Miss Amelia and Marvin confront each other as if ready to fight. When he mentions having found in the woods where he hunts a trap set for him that would have killed him, Miss Amelia admits she had set it (132). While Lymon brings in the dinner and waits on Marvin, Miss Amelia goes out and sits on the porch steps. Henry Macy joins her and tells her that Marvin will soon move on.

Act four takes place some weeks later; and, as the Narrator explains, "Henry Macy was wrong, for Marvin did not move on" (133). Instead, he stayed in the town, eating and drinking (for free) at the cafe. "Once every night" he and Miss Amelia "would circle one another, and it was during these rituals that the townspeople expected blows to be struck . . . but it never happened" (134). But "one night . . . nearly three months after Marvin Macy returned to town, there occurred an event which set the sure course to calamity" (134).

In the first of the two scenes composing act four (134–37), Miss Amelia tells Marvin to move on. He refuses. Cousin Lymon imperiously informs Amelia that Marvin is moving in, that he will sleep upstairs in her father's bed, and that he himself (Lymon) will occupy her bedroom: ". . . an' you . . . Amelia . . .

well, you can pull up a mattress an' sleep by the stove down here" (136). When they go upstairs together, Amelia is so angry that she cannot speak.

In the second scene (137–40) the townspeople—all sympathetic to Amelia—leave the cafe. Henry Macy comes outside to sit beside her, and she tells him that it is now or never: "I gotta get your brother" (138). He agrees. She would have done it long ago, she explains, except that, if she had driven Marvin off, Lymon would have gone, too—and, if he goes, she will be all alone.

> HENRY MACY: He ain't . . . much comfort, Cousin Lymon.
> MISS AMELIA: He some. He been some. I gonna get your brother, Henry.
> HENRY MACY: (*Thinks; acquiesces to it*) All right. (*Pause*) Night, Miss Amelia.
> MISS AMELIA: Night, Henry. (139)

Act five represents, in two scenes, the high point of the action, the "solemn and festive occasion" of the fight between Marvin Macy and Miss Amelia on "Ground Hog's Day" (140). The first scene (140–48) includes the preparations for the fight and the fight itself; the second, what happens immediately after the fight.

Bets have been placed by all the townspeople. "Miss Amelia had lay flat down on her porch to rest her strength for the fight"; and Marvin, sitting nearby, was greasing himself with hog fat, so she could not get a grip on him (she is greased, too) (142). During the battle, Amelia has Marvin down and is about to choke him to death. "Kill him! Kill him!" shout Mrs. Peterson and Merlie Ryan (146), but Cousin Lymon half-shrieks, half-howls, "*NNNNNNOOOOOOOOOOOO!*" and races into the melee (146.) He "*mounts Miss Amelia's back and begins choking her from behind*" (146)—an action that turns the fight in Marvin's favor, and he ruthlessly beats Miss Amelia senseless.

After the fight, scene two (148–50), the Narrator tells the audience that Marvin and Cousin Lymon then wrecked the store and left town: "They took what money there was in the cafe, and the few curios and pieces of jewelry Miss Amelia kept upstairs; and they carved vile words on the cafe tables. After they had done all this . . . they left town . . . together" (148). As we see them departing, Miss Amelia raises herself to a sitting position, howls, and then becomes silent. The stage directions call for music "*to the end of the play.*"

Albee spins out the ending with two more scenes—an Epilogue and the same scene that opens the play. In the Epilogue we learn that every night for three years Miss Amelia sat on the front steps looking down the road and waiting, "But Cousin Lymon never returned" (149). And she "closed the general store, as well, or it would be more correct to say that she discouraged anyone from coming there anymore" (149). In a brief scene Mrs. Peterson tries to buy a coke, and Amelia charges her $1.05 for it— five cents for a coke and "A dollar for lookin' at the freak" (149). Then, the Narrator relates, "Miss Amelia went indoors one night, climbed the stairs, and never again left her upstairs room" (150). At this point the large flashback ends, and we return to the present.

The Narrator concludes with the same tonal motif heard at the beginning before the flashback—again the town is "dreary," the road "empty," as the upstairs shutter opens late in the hot August afternoon and the "terrible, dim face" of Miss Amelia lingers for "an hour or so," looking down at the town: "Heat . . . and silence. There is nothing whatever to do. You might as well walk down to the Fork Falls Road and watch the chain gang. The twelve mortal men . . . who are together. The Ballad of the Sad Cafe . . . the end" (150).

II *Malcolm*

Albee's second major attempt at adapting another contemporary writer's work to the stage continued a brief downward trend in his reputation and resulted in a fiasco when his play, based on James Purdy's novel *Malcolm*, closed after only seven performances.[2] Albee nevertheless published the play as a book—whether to vindicate his contention that the play was artistically sound or merely to make more money is difficult to say.

Each of the two acts comprising *Malcolm* has nine scenes, and these in turn are interspersed with entre-scenes. The function of Act I is to describe Malcolm's life up to the time of his marriage; Act II, to the time of his death. As the curtain rises, we see Malcolm sitting on "*a golden bench*" before a hotel where Professor

Cox appears before him and introduces himself. Malcolm, who is waiting for a father who has disappeared, is as old as a boy is when hair first appears under the arms; and Cox tells him that he must leave the bench and begin his "education to life" (9). When Malcolm replies that he and his father had been "very happy together" (8), Cox urges him to prepare himself for life because he has "the look of innocence . . . and that will never do," for "innocence has the appearance of stupidity" (9). "Innocence must [therefore] go!" according to Cox, who offers to supply the names and addresses of people who will help Malcolm lose it.The first people Cox offers to introduce him to are Kermit and Laureen Raphaelson, whom Cox describes as "children—like yourself"—"Grown-up children" (11). In the following short entre-scene, Malcolm, who addresses his father in a soliloquy, explains that he misses him very much, saying that he will try to be "all you have taught me . . . polite; honest; and . . . what is the rest of it, father?" (12).

Scene two, which takes place in the Raphaelson home, shows the couple headed for the divorce court. Kermit Raphaelson claims to be "the oldest man in the world," one hundred and ninety-two years old, to be exact (15), although his wife says he is only ninety-seven (16). Kermit offers Malcolm friendship (20); but when Malcolm asks if he is not afraid of dying (because of his advanced age), he calls for his wife, whom he had previously sent to the back of the house "with the other alley cats!" (19); and they send Malcolm away. To them, he doesn't know what life is; and, besides, they want to be alone for a little while.

By way of explanation, Kermit says: "When I was your age, Malcolm, the idea of death occurred to me, and I was very frightened . . . by the time I was a hundred or so . . . I'd resigned myself to it. . . . But on my one hundred and forty-fifth birthday the idea suddenly hit me that there wasn't any death. So when I was a hundred and eighty-five I married Laureen here . . ." (23).

In the entre-scene (26–28), Professor Cox appears to Malcolm, who asserts that "of everything I have seen, married love is the strangest thing of all" (26). Malcolm cannot understand why Laureen will not admit that Kermit is one hundred and ninety-two. "The day will come," says Cox, when "Laureen will have to admit that Kermit is one hundred and ninety-two years old, or

Kermit will have to admit that he isn't." Malcolm then asks, "You mean they can't both go on believing what they want?" Cox replies, "Well, not if they're the only ones who believe it" (27). (This passage echoes the illusion-reality theme of *Virginia Woolf.*)

At the beginning of scene three Malcolm speaks to his father, asking him if he knows the Girards—the second couple whose card is given to Malcolm. "Is that where you are, father?" we hear him say. "Will you be waiting for me there?" (29). A young man then appears to Malcolm to urge him to come along as Mme Girard is "demanding a settlement from her husband; you're just in time for the evening's performance" (29). Madame Girard, who wears pancake make-up and sits on "*a throne of sorts,*" behaves imperiously despite her intoxication; and she continues drinking (30). Attended as she is by a quartet of kept young men, she nevertheless orders her husband to get Malcolm a drink. Then she suspects that Malcolm is "a filthy spy for that vicious old pederast" Professor Cox (33). Accordingly, she begs him to leave Cox and be hers—"be my own Malcolm, not his" (35).

Scene four returns us to Kermit's place. Laureen has just run off with a Japanese wrestler.

> MALCOLM: It's pretty scary, isn't it, being alone?
> KERMIT: We're both alone, you and I. Aren't we lucky Professor Cox brought us together? We're both in an impossible situation (38).

When Malcolm wants to talk about his father, Kermit offends him deeply by cursing him. Malcolm forgives him, however, when he explains that he "only meant irritation" (39).

> KERMIT: There you were, talking on and on about your father, and I wanted to talk about *myself*, and about the whore [she had been a prostitute] of a wife . . . who I miss so much. . . . (39).
> MALCOLM: (*Shyly*) Kermit? Why did Laureen really leave you?
> KERMIT: (*Sighs*) It was so strange. At exactly the same minute I decided to tell her I was only ninety-seven, to make it easier for her, she walked into the room, looking sort of funny, saying she'd decided to live with the fact that I was a hundred and ninety-two. And so we argued about it for a while, me insist-

ing I was only ninety-seven, and she telling me that I was older than hell itself, and then she said she couldn't take it any more, and . . .

MALCOLM: How . . . how old are you? Really?

KERMIT: Hm? Oh . . . well, I don't remember any more. I'm up there, though . . . two . . . two hundred and something.

MALCOLM: I . . . I like you, Kermit. I like you very much.

KERMIT: Yes? Well, come and see me soon, Malcolm. I'm really very lonely now. (40)

In the entre-scene (41–44) Malcolm encounters a streetwalker whose real name is Ethel. When he mistakes her for Laureen (she is played by the same actress) and begs her to return home to Kermit, she makes fun of him, thinking him crazy.

Scene five shows Malcolm's hotel bedroom. Girard Girard, who owns the hotel, is waiting there for him. He invites Malcolm to spend the summer with him and Madame Girard at their chateau. Malcolm accepts, provided that Kermit, his friend, can come, too. "Come spend the summer with us; be our son," Girard urges him.

MALCOLM: Be *like* your son, sir.

GIRARD GIRARD: (. . . *wistfully*) Between simile and metaphor lies all the sadness in the world, Malcolm. (48)

But as Girard Girard goes off, Cox appears, saying to Kermit, who looks forward to visiting the Girards, "Oh, I wouldn't count on that, buddy, if I were you. I wouldn't be so sure about that at all. . . . I wouldn't count on any thing in this whole damn world" (49).

In scene six, which has three parts, the first is laid in Kermit's sitting room; there Cox persuades Kermit that he "couldn't take the splendor" of the Girards' chateau (52). In the second part when the Girards come to take Kermit to the chateau, he whiningly refuses to go. Without his friend, Malcolm also refuses to go, and the Girards depart alone. In the third, Malcolm reproves Kermit in the following important speech that shows for the first time the growth of Malcolm's *selfishness*, and also of his loneliness:

(*Rather petulant*) Well, you've made rather a hash of things, I must say, Kermit. A whole summer, two people who loved me, or so they said, a man like Mr. Girard who said he would be like my

> father—all of it, everything, for *both* of us, and you won't do it! (*Tapping his foot, rather impatient*) Well? What's to become of me now? I hope you've got plans for me. I've given up everything for you! (*But* MALCOLM *is alone. Frightened little boy*) What's to become of me? (58)

The entre-scene shows Cox and Malcolm out on the street—for the boy has checked out of his hotel and is completely indigent. When Malcolm asks Cox what is going to happen to Kermit, Cox replies that Kermit is "probably going to have a nearly complete collapse . . . the presence of the unattainable often brings one on" (60). When he hands Malcolm a new address card, Malcolm, who is more confused than ever, says in "*real anger*": "I don't understand your world, Mr. Cox, sir! Not one bit!" To which Cox replies, "You will, sonny, you will," and then walks away, leaving Malcolm very much alone (62).

The first of two parts of scene seven presents, against a background of jazz music, Eloisa Brace, a bohemian painter who runs a flophouse for jazz musicians and who is considering painting Malcolm's portrait: "There's that face of yours, I'm gonna paint. (*Rather mysterious*) It's like a commission: I mean, I think I can sell it right away I got it done. O.K.?" (64). When her husband Jerome comes in, she leaves, saying she has to tend to the musicians. In part two Jerome, a writer, an ex-convict, and a burglar, offers Malcolm a glass of wine. Deceived by Jerome's politeness, Malcolm accepts it and is soon intoxicated. As Jerome attempts to seduce him, Malcolm passes out.

Scene eight (69–80) is long and is composed of four subdivisions. In the first of these we are still in Eloisa Brace's apartment, although at a later time. She has just painted Malcolm's portrait, which she hopes to sell to Madame Girard. Acting as agent in this transaction, Cox (who will get a 15 per cent commission) says: "Madame Girard finds herself in the curious dilemma of, on the one hand, feeling that Malcolm is the most ungrateful child who ever lived, and, on the other hand, retaining for the boy—or, to put it most accurately, for the fact of him—a possessiveness that borders on mania" (70).

In the second part (71–74) Madame Girard's voice is heard and Cox disappears, leaving the two women alone. They talk of their mutual interest in Malcolm, who apparently is staying in Eloisa's establishment. Whatever the place is—a private house, public house, house of prostitution, or merely a flophouse—Albee never quite makes clear; but we do learn that there is a good deal of shifting around in the middle of the night and three-in-a-bed sleeping because, as Eloisa says, "it's a little crowded around here—what with musicians coming and going at all hours—and there aren't enough beds" (74).

When Madame Girard asks Malcolm if he has lost his innocence in this establishment, he admits it is a little crowded at bedtime—"like traveling in Czechoslovakia during a war" (74). At almost the same moment Girard Girard arrives unexpectedly—just back from Idaho and from making six million dollars there. He informs Madame Girard that he now plans to divorce her and to marry Laureen Raphaelson. She (Madame Girard) may have "the mansion and the chateau" and wealth enough to satisfy her "every whim" as long as she gives back his name. When she asks "what will become of me?" Girard Girard "(*A little weary, a little sad*)" replies: "You will move from the mansion to the chateau and from the chateau back. You will surround yourself with your beauties, and hide your liquor where you will. You will . . . go on, my dear" (79).

Madame Girard grabs the portrait and each runs off in opposite directions, leaving Malcolm alone at the curtain (part four) to say: "everything I touch is . . . each place I go, the . . . the, THE WHOLE WORLD IS FLYING APART!! The . . . the whole world is . . . Have . . . Have I done this? Is . . . is this because of me? I've been polite, and honest, and . . . I've *tried.* I don't understand the world. No, I don't understand it at all. I feel that thing, father . . . Loss. Loss . . . father?" (80).

In Eloisa's studio in scene nine, she and Jerome tell Malcolm they are closing their establishment; and they very delicately let him know that he must move. They have just received a ten-thousand-dollar check from Madame Girard for the portrait of Malcolm; furthermore, Jerome had himself picked up a tidy thirty-five hundred dollars for the sale of Malcolm *himself* to Mr. Girard Girard, who is now waiting for him at the entrance to the botanical gardens. Now Malcolm's world flies apart more than ever as he realizes he has been really "sold." Alone at the curtain of the act, he says, " SOLD? SOLD? The . . . THE WHOLE WORLD IS FLYING APART! And . . . what's to become of me? WHAT'S TO BECOME OF ME NOW!!??" (86).

At the beginning of the second act, Malcolm is asleep at the entrance to the botanical gardens. Instead of Girard, a character by the name of Gus, described as "*tall, brawny, [and] got up in motorcycle uniform*" (89), wakes him and talks to him about Melba, the jazz singer whose recording "You Said Goodbye, Dark Daddy," had sold eight million records (92). Apparently, Melba had asked Gus to find her a "contemporary," and once again in the game of catch-as-catch-can Malcolm is it (92–93).

In the second scene we go backstage of a club where Melba is singing—"*we hear screaming from 'onstage,' and we hear* MELBA *singing, vaguely; what we hear mostly is applause and screaming*" (94). Melba, instantly attracted to Malcolm, kisses him many times and wants to marry him, and Malcolm wants to marry her. Gus, her first husband, warns her against marriage, speaking of "all the other times" she had "done got stung" (98). The emotional effect of this scene is compounded of shock and surprise at the rapidity with which Melba wants to marry this boy whom she has just met. Similarly, the surprise effect is intensified, or rather doubled, by Malcolm's immediate acceptance of her proposal and by his obvious enjoyment of her passionate kisses. At the end of the scene Melba tells Gus to "take good care of, uh, Malcolm here, ya hear? (*Waving at* MALCOLM, *blowing him a kiss. Sotto voce to* GUS, *taking money from her bodice, giving it to* GUS) Mature him up a little, you know? You know what I mean? Mature him up a little (MELBA *exits, the crowd sounds swell.*)" (100).

In the entre-scene, Malcolm and Gus are walking, but Malcolm is still dazed by the suddenness of his forthcoming marriage to Melba whom he is unable to resist. For Gus, however, despite a few flutterings of the torch he still carries for Melba, this marriage is purely a business transaction; and he quickly gets down to brass tacks:

> GUS: To put it delicate-like, boy, have you ever been completely and solidly joined to a woman? Have you ever been joined to a woman the way nature meant? Yes or no.
>
> MALCOLM (*After a puzzled pause*): Well, it's always been so very dark—where I was—and people were—shifting so . . .
>
> GUS: I can see you ain't, and that's what Melba meant—what she sent us out for, to mature you up. (103)

Consequently, Gus takes Malcolm in scene three to a place advertising "PRIVATE AND TURKISH BATHS. CABINETS AND OVERNIGHT COTTAGES $2.00" (104)—in reality, Mme Rosita's house of prostitution. Here they meet Miles, whom Malcolm mistakes for Cox. (Albee bases such confusion on similiarity of function; as noted earlier, Malcolm mistakes the whore Mme Rosita for Laureen Raphaelson, also one; and he mistakes Miles, a panderer, for Cox, the alleged pederast.) In the whorehouse Miles notices that Malcolm is "sorta young"—fifteen, to be exact (108). But, when Gus waves Melba's money under Miles's nose, he reconsiders: "Yeah, well, looks is deceiving" (105).

In scene four Malcolm is parting from Mme Rosita, who is thoroughly satisfied and who has given him a going-away present of a locket with "a real, little tiny American flag all rolled up inside." All "matured up," Malcolm is now delivered to Melba, who suggests they run off to Chicago to get married. "Why Chicago?" asks Malcolm.

MELBA: You ever been married in Chicago?
MALCOLM: Well . . . no!
MELBA: Well, neither have I, baby! Let's go! (*They race off together*). (110)

In the entre-scene, "*another no-set promenade,*" Madame Girard comes on, followed by Kermit, and they stroll (111). Mme Girard's letters to Malcolm, we learn, had been answered by Melba, who writes that Malcolm was "busy at being married, . . . too occupied and happy to be . . . dragged under by his past!" Kermit's antagonism toward Mme Girard is evident in this little scene in which she does all the talking, for he—a sympathetic character—realizes that she has been a party to what he considers Malcolm's ruin. Although he says nothing, she senses his antagonism and accuses him of being responsible because he had not come along with them on the earlier summer trip to the chateau. Of course, she has Malcolm's portrait, but it is little consolation. At the end of the scene she moans, "Get me my Malcolm back!" (112), but Kermit walks away from her.

In scene five, something of a *scène à faire,* Malcolm and Melba are in bed together. He is giggling because she is tickling him. Heliodoro, the Cuban valet, interrupts their rather heavy love play—of which Malcolm, incidentally, is beginning to weary—

by announcing that it is time for Melba to go to work. In her murderous bullying of Heliodoro, which alternates with her over-possessive, tender lovemaking towards Malcolm, she appears completely absurd. This scene shows Malcolm completely enslaved by Melba but beginning to weary of her incessant attentions; he is her kept man.

The entre-scene (118–21) is devoted to high-toned business rhetoric from the Braces to cover up the customer's dissatisfaction after they have pocketed his money. Eloisa and Jerome Brace, a pair of richly comic characters, portray honor among thieves by acting offended that Girard Girard should have expressed regret at not finding Malcolm at the entrance to the botanical gardens when he had arrived there some hours later—having been detained because of business. They accuse him of having accused them and pretend to be deeply offended.

In scene six, which marks the beginning of the end, Malcolm and Melba are at a nightclub table; and they are beginning to tire of each other. When Malcolm sees a man he thinks is his father, he follows him into the washroom (scene seven) and grapples with him in an attempt to have himself recognized. The man calls for help from an attendant and then in exasperation throws Malcolm to the floor, so that he cuts his head. In the second part of the scene Malcolm babbles to the washroom attendant about his father, whose existence he had come to doubt yet still hoped for (128); but, as the attendant explains to Malcolm, that man had been coming there for years and was "nobody's father" (127). The attendant tries to get Malcolm to a doctor before he bleeds to death from the cut on his head.

In the first of two parts in scene eight, Mme Girard calls on Melba, attempting to wrest from her the custody of Malcolm, who, she insists, is only a fifteen-year-old child. In the second, the doctor comes in to announce that Malcolm is dying of "a combination of acute alcoholism and sexual hyperaesthesia" (133). Melba leans for support on Heliodoro, as she says to him, "This just ain't a good day. Old Malcolm's gonna die. He's gonna leave us" (134).

The last scene presents the death of Malcolm. Not yet twenty by his own admission (135), he feels abandoned by all his friends. Mme Girard bewails Malcolm's passing, saying, "My Malcolm. What have you not lost? . . . And I . . . And all . . . What have *we* not lost? What, indeed. Did none of us ever care?" Then, after the other "friends" have grouped themselves around his bed, she promises to "have a fine funeral for him! A silver casket? Banks of roses and violets? Thousands and thousands of . . . and a gilded hearse? With black-plumed horses?" (137). She accuses them of not having cared; but when they say they did care, she invites them to come to see his portrait if they cared: "That's all that's left" (138).

The final stage direction, a combination of corny apotheosis and theatrical cliché, reads as follows: "*As the lights fade on* MADAME GIRARD *and the dead* MALCOLM, *they rise on the garden bench, high on a platform, above and behind. The bench is suffused in a golden light for a few moments, then all fades to blackness*" (138).

No discussion of this kind could ever be complete, of course, without Albee's own statement about transforming works in other genres for stage production. The following quotation, which appeared in the *New York Times* on the eve of the production of *Malcolm*, is from his article on James Purdy, the author of the novel:

> Adaptation can be a perfectly respectable occupation for a playwright and, more important, a valid artistic act. And, naturally, no self-respecting playwright would, unless the roof were falling in on him and his, set about to adapt anything which (1) he did not respect as a work of art and (2) which he did not feel to be in line with his own esthetic. . . .
>
> One of the greater pleasures I received when I made the adaptation of Carson McCullers' "The Ballad of the Sad Cafe" was to be thanked for putting dialogue from the book so faithfully on the stage when, in truth, the book is without dialogue. . . . the pleasure of working on "The Ballad of the Sad Cafe" far outweighed the sorrows . . . and the fact that the piece was far more of a critical success than a commercial one is just so much of a shrug.
>
> With James Purdy's book, I have wandered further, in specifics, than I did with McCullers', but I have come as far back. . . .[3]

While granting the truth of everything that Albee here says, many would nevertheless incline to the view that Walter Kerr expressed when he wrote, "On the evidence of 'Ballad of the Sad Cafe' and 'Malcolm,' it would seem that Mr. Albee's announced intention of alternating adaptations with new plays of his own is a misguided one."[4] As a kind of postscript to this matter, newspaper reports indicate that the most recent of Albee's adaptations has just closed in New York after a run of about two and a half months. I did not have a chance to see this play, and, as my manuscript goes to print, the play has not yet been published. But one reviewer took issue with Albee's statement that he had completely reworked Giles Cooper's play *Everything in the Garden* and also made the point that Albee's play was "*not* so good as the original."[5]

CHAPTER 9

Experiment in Surrealism

OF ALL THE PLAYS written by Albee, *Tiny Alice* (1964) is as yet his most daring and original experiment in pure theater. It embodies many ideas of Antonin Artaud and the Balinese theater that served as Artaud's source, including the Indonesian concept of *Wayang*, a word which means "shadow." "Originally the wayang play was a religious act executed by the head of the family to invite the spirits of the ancestors, when their advice was needed before important events such as a marriage . . . [T]he spirit appeared in the form of a shadow." It can also mean the revelation of spiritual inspiration and the dalang, or all-purpose narrator, also has as his function the "unfolding of widsom."[1]

Much of the befuddlement that readers and playgoers have encountered in attempting to read meaning into the play, or to make sense out of it, is due to mistaken efforts to reduce the play to a philosophical tract, to a straight psychological study of character, or to a mere allegory.[2] Albee himself has referred to the play as "something of a metaphysical dream play which must be entered into and experienced without preconception of how a play is supposed to go."[3] The sources for the play, besides those already mentioned, may be traced back to the French theater and seen against a background of Surrealism—and possibly of Existentialism.[4] Here, as with other experimental plays, the best prerequisite for understanding is an open mind.

I *Albee's Remarks*

Albee's own summary of the plot of this play is so succinct and cogent that it must surely take precedence over any other analysis:

> TINY ALICE is a fairly simple play, and not at all unclear, once you approach it on its own terms. The story is simply this:

> A lay brother, a man who would have become a priest except that he could not reconcile his idea of God with the God which men create in their own image, is sent by his superior to tie up loose ends of a business matter between the church and a wealthy woman. The lay brother becomes enmeshed in an environment which, at its core and shifting surface, contains all the elements which have confused and bothered him throughout his life: the relationship between sexual hysteria and religious ecstasy; the conflict between selflessness of service and the conspicuous splendor of martyrdom. The lay brother is brought to the point, finally, of having to accept what he had insisted he wanted . . . union with the abstraction, rather than [a] man-made image of it, its substitution. He is left with pure abstraction—whatever it be called: God, or Alice—and in the end, according to your faith, one of two things happens: either the abstraction personifies itself, is proved real, or the dying man, in the last necessary effort of self-delusion[,] creates and believes in what he knows does not exist.
>
> It is, you see, a perfectly straightforward story, dealt with in terms of reality and illusion, symbol and actuality. It is the very simplicity of the play, I think, that has confused so many.[5]

Albee then pleads for a fair hearing, for letting the play "happen to one," for letting "the mind loose to respond as it will, to receive impressions without immediately categorizing them, to sense rather than to know, to gather rather than immediately understand." "If the play is approached in this way, the experience of it will be quite simple. If, on the other hand, one is instructed to follow the allegory as it moves, to count and relate the symbols, then, of course, the result is confusion, opacity, difficulty . . . all the things the play has been accused of . . . [M]y instruction to anyone who wanted to see the play would be this: sit back, let it happen to you, and take it rather as you would a piece of music or a dream."[6] Again, in the Author's Note to the play, Albee insists that "the play is quite clear"; but he does admit that it is "less opaque in reading than it would be in any single viewing." Certain deletions, especially in the final act, were made for the acting version, which he restored in the text of the printed play.[7]

II *Analysis of the Text*

The text of the play has Act I divided into three main scenes, which we can subdivide if we remember our definition of a scene as any regrouping of characters, or if we look for tonal or logical shifts in the subject matter being presented. Scene one of the first act, for example, illustrates rather well the second kind of subdividing. The function of the scene as a whole is to announce a bequest of money to the church and to characterize the Lawyer and the Cardinal.

The Lawyer announces the bequest to the Cardinal and, in the process, the exceedingly corrupt characters of both are revealed. The intent is clearly to satirize the institutions each represents—the church and the legal profession—or, roughly, the man-made image of the divine law, and the secular, or civil, law, both of which, in conjunction with Miss Alice's wealth and power, ultimately bring about the bad fortune of Brother Julian, the Cardinal's secretary. The first part of scene one takes place in the Cardinal's garden; there the Lawyer, alone, is talking to two birds, cardinals, in an elaborate cage. When the Cardinal appears, the two men join in mutually insulting each other; and they become increasingly sarcastic with each other, possibly because of a homosexual attachment the two shared when they were boys attending the same school (10–13).

Following this scene, there is an abrupt change in tone as the Cardinal quietly says, "And now that we have brought the past to mind, and remembered what we could not exactly, shall we . . . talk business?" (12). But the Lawyer, pursuing his own line of thought, only says, "Robes the color of your mother's vice" (12). This sentence recalls his earlier characterization of the Cardinal as an "Overstuffed, arrogant, pompous son of a profiteer. And a whore" (9). The Lawyer's mind then jumps to the bird cage, as he wonders if the two birds (cardinals) therein are lovers. And from there he jumps again to the discussion of homosexuality already alluded to—concerning the boys' school.

Now, however, the Cardinal insists on talking business. Finally, they both get down to business with the announcement of the bequest. The Lawyer reveals that his client, a "youngish" lady, being "overburdened with wealth," wants to give the church one hundred million dollars immediately and the same amount annually for the next twenty years (14–17). The bequest was only one of several others—the others going to the Protestants, the Jews, "hospitals, universities, orchestras, revolutions here and there . . ." (15). The Cardinal is so astonished at the extraordinary grandeur of the bequest that he lapses into the use of *I* instead of his customary *we*—a lapse for which the Lawyer taunts him.

At the end of the scene, the Lawyer mentions his employer, Miss Alice, and her desire for privacy in this matter. Therefore the Cardinal's secretary, Brother Julian, a lay brother and not a regular priest, is nominated as the emissary to take care of the arrangements to transfer the money from Miss Alice to the church. Thus the function of this first scene also includes, in addition to what has already been mentioned, the introduction of the character who becomes the protagonist, Brother Julian. The scene closes with the Cardinal cooing affectionate nonsense to the cardinals in the cage, just as the Lawyer had at the opening of the scene. On the heels of the discussion about homosexuality among the cardinals, this little stage business before the bird cage reinforces the characterization of the Cardinal as an essentially depraved man.

The second scene continues characterization, introducing Brother Julian and the Butler to the audience and giving another glimpse of the nefarious Lawyer whom the Cardinal, in anger, had called "Satan" in scene one (19). Scene two has three parts. In the first (23–31), we see Brother Julian and the Butler talking about the miniature model of the castle in which Miss Alice lives and admiring the model's workmanship. Then in part two (31–42), when the Lawyer comes in, they talk about the six-year blank period in Brother Julian's life; but he refuses to divulge the details in the presence of the Lawyer, whom he instantly dislikes. In part three, after the Lawyer leaves, Julian tells the Butler about this period of his life (42–45).

This entire second scene takes place in "*the library of a mansion—a castle.*" Besides the "*floor-to-ceiling leather-bound books*" and other trappings, the most "*essential*" part of the set is the "*huge doll's-house model of the building of which the present room [the library] is a part*" (23)— the remarkable model which fascinates Julian. Even the Butler "*who moves about with a kind of unbutlerlike ease*" never ceases to wonder at it, he says—particularly at the fact that the castle is duplicated in "such precise miniature." He calls Julian's attention to the exactness of detail, to the fact that the model contains a room exactly like the room they themselves now occupy in the mansion. He teases Julian by asking him if there is anyone in the miniature. Startled, Julian inspects the model anew, but finds no one there. To which the Butler replies: "One feels one should see one's self . . . almost." Julian answers, "*after a brief thoughtful pause,*" "Yes. That would be rather a shock, wouldn't it?" With remarkable tenacity the Butler presses Julian, asking if he had noticed that there is a model within the model itself. "You don't suppose," he continues, "that within that tiny model in the model there, there is . . . another room like this, with yet a tinier model within it, and within . . ." (25). Julian picks up this idea with a laugh, ". . . and within and within and within and . . .? No, I . . . rather doubt it. It's remarkable craftsmanship, though. Remarkable" (26).

Now, while Albee has specifically warned against a strictly allegorical interpretation of the play in an attempt to reduce it to pure meaning, we must not overlook the fact that in dreams, at the level of unconscious thinking, the mind sometimes expresses itself by the use of symbols, particularly to soften unpleasant aspects of its experience. Here, I think, the model is a symbol, as perhaps the mansion within which it rests also is; and I suggest that together they symbolize the universe—the mansion being the macrocosm; the model, the microcosm.

If so, what is Albee hinting at? The logic of the passage would indicate his belief that the microcosm, the unexplored tiny world, might be just as *infinitely small* as the macrocosm (the world of starry space) is increasingly found to be *infinitely large,* at least for our little minds. And, if we look for deity in the macrocosm, which we ourselves inhabit, why should we not also go prospecting for it in the microcosm, which we don't inhabit—the world within the model, where, as we discover later in the play, *Tiny* Alice, as distinct from *Miss* Alice, the inordinately wealthy owner of the mansion, lives? I pose this question simply because Albee himself has referred to *Tiny Alice* as "a metaphysical dream play"[8] and because the handling of the conversation between the Butler and Julian in this scene suggests something more than mere conversation.

Since the second part of this scene is too long—it really does very little to advance the action beyond showing Julian's aversion to the Satanic Lawyer and providing a few snappy swipes by the Lawyer at the Church and the Cardinal—we proceed to the third part of the scene, wherein, after the Lawyer departs, Julian explains to the Butler what happened to him during the six-year period in question. The Butler is as much a chorus as this play offers, but he also turns out to be the confidant of Julian. His first comment, one which wins Julian to his side, is to characterize the Lawyer as a "Nasty man." There is little love lost between the Lawyer and the Butler (though they do address each other as sweetheart, from time to time—probably in irony or in some kind of cynical homosexual play). We learn later that they have both been lovers of Miss Alice (55), who calls the Butler "gentle" and the Lawyer "pig" (55).

Asked by the Butler about the six years in his thirties concerning which the Lawyer has been unable to procure information, Julian explains very simply that he had lost his faith in God, had consequently suffered a kind of nervous breakdown, and had institutionalized himself in a mental home:

> JULIAN: I could not reconcile myself to the chasm between the nature of God and the use to which men put . . . God.
> BUTLER: Between your God and others', your view and theirs.
> JULIAN: I said what I intended (*Weighs the opposites in each hand*): It is God the mover, not God the puppet; God the creator, not the God created by man.
> BUTLER (*Almost pitying*): Six years in the loony bin for semantics?
> JULIAN (*Slightly flustered, heat*): It is not semantics! Men create a false God in their own image, it is easier for them! . . . It is not . . ." (44)

At this moment the chime sounds, signifying that Miss Alice will see Julian and the Butler. As they move off to her upstairs tower apartment, Julian remarks, "My faith and my sanity . . . they are one and the same" (45). To which the Butler smiles noncommittally as they exit and the scene ends.

Scene three, the last in Act I, also has three parts. In the first the Lawyer is present with Miss Alice while the Butler brings Julian to them. As Miss Alice sits in a large wing chair with her back to the audience, we don't at first see her; but the Lawyer mentions that she is very hard of hearing and equally slow of reply because of her advanced age. Since Julian had been prepared to discover a young woman, he now finds Miss Alice somewhat of an enigma, as does the audience. She rises slowly from her chair and comes around it: "*Her face is that of a withered crone, her hair gray and white and matted; she is bent; she moves with two canes.*" And she speaks with "*a cracked and ancient voice*" (48).

After shouting at her for a while, the Lawyer leaves Julian alone with her. She briefly continues this playacting and then strips herself of her wig, canes, and mask, and stands before the astonished Julian as a really beautiful young woman. She tells him that "it's only a little game . . . a little lightness to counter the weight" (52–53). For, as she explains, they are "involved in weighty matters . . . the transfer of millions, the rocking of empires . . ." (53). She asks him his impressions of the Butler and the Lawyer, then explains that the "gentle" Butler had once been her lover, but that now she is mistress of the Lawyer of whom, incidentally, she is now tired. She too asks about the six-year gap in Julian's dossier. He replies just as simply and directly as he had to the Butler that his faith in God had left him and that he had had himself committed to an asylum.

When she asks how many women he has slept with, he replies "I am not certain" (59). When she finds this a very strange answer, he recounts the even stranger history of an episode that had occurred to him in the asylum. Because he had been subject to hallucinations—strange ringing and roaring sounds, he could not be certain whether the overwhelming sex experience (61–62) he *thought* he had there with a female patient had really happened or not. At any rate, the woman had subsequently regarded herself as "pregnant with the Son of God." When he consulted his doctor about her, he discovered that she was suffering from an advanced cancer of the womb. "In a month, she died" (64). When he asks Miss Alice if he has answered her question, she, puzzled, slowly replies: "I don't . . . know. Is the memory of something having happened the same as it[s] having happened?" (65). This question, closely connected with the *Virginia Woolf* theme of illusion versus reality, may provide one key to understanding the play as a whole.[9]

After probing Julian's psyche and past, Miss Alice tells Brother Julian a little about herself: "I am rich and beautiful and I live here in all these rooms . . . without relatives, with a . . . (*Wry*) companion, from time to time . . . (*Leans forward, whispers, but still amused*) . . . and with a secret" (65). When Julian asks if he may know her secret, she says she does not know—yet! Immediately there occurs one of the swift changes of mood we have already observed between the Cardinal and the Lawyer in scene one (12). Miss Alice turns on her brisk, official coolness and wants to talk business (65). Then, while terminating the interview, she goes so far as to suggest that Julian move into the mansion, kisses him on the forehead, and says "I'll send for you, we'll have . . . pleasant afternoons, you and I. Goodby" (68). She gazes out the window as Julian exits and the Lawyer enters.

In the third part, which is very brief, the Lawyer asks when she intends seeing Julian again. She answers "Whenever you like, whenever you say." Then, in a serious tone, she asks, "Tell me honestly, do you really think we're wise?" He replies, "Wise? Well, we'll see. If we prove not, I can't think of anything standing in the way that can't be destroyed. . . . Can you?" Since the "anything" could refer to Julian, the curtain at this point (the end of the act) rings in a rather ominous hint of preparation, particularly as she answers "*rather sadly*": "No. Nothing" (68). We can only guess that the Lawyer's motive, in this glib talk of destruction, must be hatred of the Cardinal and what he stands for—the Church. By striking at the Cardinal's personal secretary, the Lawyer can deliver what he considers a blow of maximum devastation to the Cardinal and the institution he represents.

The seduction of Brother Julian, begun in Act I, now proceeds and is accomplished as the main business in Act II. The second act, like the first, has three scenes, the first of which is the longest and possibly the most important. In this first scene there are five subscenes or parts. In the first part (71-77), we see the Lawyer, now jealous of Julian, making love to Alice, while she repulses him. (The Butler has meanwhile taken Julian on a tour of the wine cellar.) The second part (77–81) occurs when the Butler joins the Lawyer and Alice. We now see her apparently in love with Julian (78–79), and we also gather that the Butler likes Julian, who is helping him in his work. Too, we are informed that the wine cellar is in bad condition (80).

In the third part Julian comes in and refers to the wretched condition of both the chapel and wine cellar: "One or two spiders have been busy around the altar, and the organ is . . . in need of use . . . but it *is* a chapel, a good one. The wine cellar, however . . . (*Shakes his head*) . . . great, great shame" (83). Miss Alice talks of having the wine cellar repaired, and the conversation drifts to such topics as the origin of the communion wine and the corruption of the Church and the clergy (84), the origin of the mansion in England and its relation to the model resting within it. As the Lawyer scolds Miss Alice to show Julian his power over her, Julian peers into the model to discover that the chapel is burning.

The men rush off to put out the fire in the chapel of the actual mansion. Left alone, Miss Alice, in part four, prays that the chapel may be saved, and her voice is alternately incantatory and natural. When using her natural voice, she speaks as though giving "*the suggestion of talking to someone in the model*" (92). In the fifth and last part (92–96), Julian, having helped put out the fire in the chapel of the mansion, returns to discover that the fire in the model is also out. In short, Miss Alice's prayer has been answered; and both she and Julian shiver together in fear at the same thought, which has occurred to each—that something or someone is apparently inhabiting the model.

To understand the third and fourth parts of this scene, we must examine more closely a kind of double thematic development that is occurring in them. First, with respect to the relation between the model and the mansion in which it rests, we should note carefully the use of the word "*replica*" in connection with the mansion. A *replica* is "a reproduction, facsimile, or copy (as of a picture or statue [or building]) done by the maker of the original or under his direction." More broadly, it is defined as "a facsimile of an original work of art." And the point is clearly established by the Lawyer that the mansion is a *replica* of the *model* (85), even though earlier in the play the Butler had indicated that the *model* had been made *after* the actual castle was built (24). Julian had thought at first that the mansion was a copy (hence a replica) of a similar one in England; but Miss Alice sets him straight on this point—the whole mansion had been moved—"every stone, marked and shipped" (85). Shipped where? Albee does not say; he carefully avoids any indication of time or country in the entire play, only permitting himself one reference to a "ninety-six"-degree warm day (36).

But more important than the surrealistic quality of the setting is the turn the discussion takes (86–87) when the Butler surprises Julian by asking whether they are at that very moment standing in the model *or* the replica and when the Lawyer further confuses Julian by stating that he need not necessarily accept the Butler's "alternative . . . that since we are clearly not in a model we must be in a replica" (86). The Lawyer adds that the problem they are discussing depends, rather, on their "concept of reality, on the limit of possibilities . . ." (87). Here, then, we are clearly back again on the theme of the ambiguous borderline between illusion and reality that Albee has treated in *Who's Afraid of Virginia Woolf?* and that has occupied so prominent a position in so much of Genet's work.[10]

Second, we must surely ask what Albee's intention is in making Miss Alice speak with two different voices in part four of this scene, especially as he indicates that she is to use her *natural* voice when addressing the supposed presence within the model, and an entirely different voice—her incantatory tone (91)—when praying to God. And we may also ask: To what extent does this dual address to two different deities connect with Julian's earlier statement of the cause of his breakdown—his failure to reconcile himself "to the chasm between the nature of God and the use to which men put . . . God." The difference is between "God the mover" and "God the puppet," the latter being a false God created by men in their own image, because doing so is, to use Julian's word, "easier" (44).

The last two scenes of Act II are relatively simple. In scene two the Lawyer and the Butler, alone together in the library of the mansion, discuss the progress of the love affair between Julian and Miss Alice. The Lawyer, who appears exceedingly jealous of Julian, thinks of going again to see the Cardinal to inform him of developments. He and the Butler engage in a bit of horseplay, the Lawyer pretending he is the Cardinal; the Butler, that he is the Lawyer.[11] In the horseplay the Butler informs the Lawyer (acting as Cardinal) that Brother Julian is about to be taken away from the service of the church, and the Lawyer takes grim satisfaction in the thought that the real Cardinal will be greatly shocked to hear that Julian is leaving ecclesiastical service to marry a wealthy woman. "It will blanch his goddam robes . . . turn'em white," he says, to hear the whole story (103).

But the whole story is apparently something more than the

marriage of Julian to Miss Alice, for the Butler points to the model and says to the Lawyer; "And I suppose you'd better tell him [the Cardinal] about... this, too" (104). The Butler then thinks "it would be a lovely touch [of irony] were the Cardinal to marry them, to perform the wedding, to marry Julian to...

> LAWYER: Alice.
> BUTLER: *Miss* Alice.
> LAWYER: Alice!
> BUTLER: Well, all right; one through the other. But have him marry them. (104)

Superficially considered, the Lawyer's motive for insisting that Julian marry Alice (in the model) rather than Miss Alice (the flesh-and-blood woman in the mansion) is, of course, that he himself is in love with Miss Alice and therefore has no scruples about getting rid of Julian. More basically, however, the Lawyer and Julian are at war with each other because of what they are, what they represent—cold *reason* and warm *faith*, respectively.[12]

The Butler nevertheless has the last word in this passage, for he comes up with a compromise—have Julian marry *them both*, bring him into union with Alice through marriage to Miss Alice. The *reasonableness* of this solution appeals to the Lawyer, who accepts it with a smile, saying that "It would be nice" (105). It might be objected that, considering his interest in Miss Alice, this acceptance of her marriage to Julian constitutes an inconsistency on the Lawyer's part. But Albee cleverly covers his tracks, even at this superficial level, by showing the Lawyer angry at the thought of Julian's hands on Miss Alice (108–9), and then by having him mollified by the Butler's telling him that the union of Julian and Miss Alice will be only "temporary" and that the Lawyer will ultimately "have her back."

Again following the Butler (103), the Lawyer asks, "But *shall* we tell him the whole thing? The Cardinal? What is happening?"

> BUTLER: How much can he take?
> LAWYER: He is a man of God, however much he simplifies, however much he worships the *symbol* and not the *substance*. (105) [My italics]

Surely these are the two key terms of the play—*symbol* and *substance*. The anthropomorphic god that Julian objects to and that the Cardinal, with his great interest in the outward trappings of the Church represents, is, of course, merely the symbol, not the substance. The God that most men invent in their own image, "the older brother, scout leader . . . Gingerbread God with the raisin eyes" (106), and that comforts most men can never be acceptable to Julian because this God is the symbol rather than the substance. Or, to put it more accurately, it is the *illusion* rather than the *reality;* it is not the true God, not the purified abstraction. And since we began with the model rather than the mansion, it is the tiny Alice that inhabits the model—as distinct from the life-size, flesh-and-blood *Miss* Alice who lives in the mansion—that ultimately becomes the *real* one, since it is reality we are searching for. The term *real* here obviously stems from a basically "Platonic" point of view in which the external world of material objects is the world of illusion and in which the true or *real* world is the world of *abstract ideas,* the world of pure forms, of which the world of change, of external material things, is a mere shadow or a mirror-like reflection in terms of ultimate, eternal (unchanging) value.

Both the Butler and the Lawyer are aware that Julian in his present state of attraction to Miss Alice stands in a precarious position, one of delicate balance. He is, as the Butler says, "walking on the edge of an abyss, but is balancing. Can be pushed . . . over, back to the asylums," if he again loses his faith. "Or," as the Lawyer adds, "over . . . to the Truth" (106).

The Lawyer now takes up the playacting a second time, still retaining his role as the Cardinal (which, as Julian's superior, he enjoys); and the Butler now acts as Julian himself. The virtue of this procedure is that it dramatizes for the audience Julian's steadfastness of faith (which both the Butler and the Lawyer are doing their best to shake in one way or another) at the same time that the audience knows Julian is beginning to be tempted from his vow of chastity by Miss Alice as he is picnicking or riding with her. The Lawyer's snide references to Alice as "the mouse in the model" and as a mere toy show clearly his intention to detach Julian from his faith in the purified abstraction, the Platonic reality, that for Julian constitutes the true God. "Cut off from it, Julian, ease yourself, ease off," the Lawyer urges him (107). At the same time, somewhat contradictorily as in a dream, he persuades him to "accept it."

What does this passage mean? As I read it, they are attempting to dissuade him from expanding or personifying his abstract sense of the deity, such personification having to do with his idea of what Miss Alice, shortly to be his bride, is like. Rather, they want him to limit or demean his already abstract sense of the deity, to make even tinier this already tiny deity—the Alice in the model—to demean it to the level of a toy or a mouse. In short, they are urging him to accept the idea that the deity in the universe is a very tiny entity indeed. Reduction of the deity to a point of near nonexistence is not the same thing as positing a "Gingerbread God," worshipped by ordinary men; but it is equally unacceptable to Julian. And yet, ironically, it is tiny Alice—the minute divinity—that eventually he is married to and accepts (190).

As I interpret the play, Albee is dramatizing, in effect, not the God-is-dead idea but rather his opposition to certain Satanic forces and persons that, in the world we inhabit, have attempted to reduce God to something infinitely small and powerless. And if Julian persists in his faith—if he refuses conversion to the so-called "reasonable" symbol, the illusion, the "comforts" of the Satanic Lawyer, the limited and demeaned toy god—then what? If Julian cannot accept this concept of deity, then "*Out* with him," says the Lawyer ominously with a shrug. The probability that Julian will *not* voluntarily accept is set up by the Butler's lament, "Poor, poor Julian" (108) and by the Lawyer's final curtain speech, where he walks over to the model and, addressing it, says, "*quietly but forcefully* . . . Rest easy; you'll have him . . . Hum; purr; breathe; rest. You will have your Julian. Wait for him. He will be yours" (109). Here the Lawyer has reversed his metaphor; no longer is Alice (in the model) the toy mouse—she has become the cat; and Julian, her prey.

Consequently, this prediction of the Lawyer comes true at the end of the next scene, which shows the seduction of Julian by Miss Alice. Two or three features of this scene deserve attention. Back from riding, which they both have enjoyed, he reminisces about riding as a young boy, about the hairy nature of the groom, which, at Miss Alice's prompting, he passes off as the "mental sex play" of unconscious youth (113). Miss Alice inquires about the state of his bodily hair, compares herself to a horse he is riding, and wishes to know if he is enjoying his stay in the mansion. One or two matters have disturbed him, he replies; gluttony "has many faces," he reminds her; "we can have too much . . . of comfort, of surroundings, of ease, of kindness . . . of happiness. I am filled to bursting" (116). She retaliates that he is there in service of the Church. He has not lost sight of this fact, he replies; but he also feels that in some manner he is being tested, being tempted.

Then he speaks of his youthful ardent desires for self-sacrifice, his longing "to be of great service," even for martyrdom (118–19). When she opines that martyrs were only "death seekers and hysterics" and that Joan of Arc was "only one of the suicides," he quivers with intensity and says, "I WISH TO SERVE AND . . . BE FORGOTTEN" (121). She tries to persuade him that he is presently "*do*ing great service," arguing that "had some lesser man than you come, some bishop, all dried and salted, clacketing phrases from memory, or . . . one of those insinuating super-salesmen your Church uses, had one of them come . . . who knows? Perhaps the whole deal would have gone out of the window" (122). She then says that he is "being used"; moreover, she, too, is (123).

Then, as he further expatiates on his youthful vivid dreams of martyrdom, of being crushed by a lion like the early Christians in the Roman arenas, she whispers into his ear, "Marry me, Julian" (124). His hallucinatory vision fuses death from the powerful bite of a lion with being throttled by a gladiator, and both of these are mingled with his earlier memory of a sexual experience with a deluded woman in the asylum (125, 61). Miss Alice's whispered pleadings of "Marry me," however, soon change to such phrases as "Come to Alice, Julian, in your sacrifice . . . give yourself to her. . . . Alice says she wants you, come to Alice, Alice tells me so. . . . Alice tells me so, instructs me, come to her."

When he utters "*a sort of dying cry*" (127) and moves into her arms, in the unfurled gown she wears like great wings and wraps about him, she soothes him with the thought that he will be "hers" and that he is a sacrifice to *her*. *Her* in this context obviously refers to Alice (of the model); but it is by means of Miss Alice, acting as an agent, as instrument, that this union is brought about. Then, as Miss Alice sets up a great cry of victory at the curtain, we realize that the Lawyer's prophecy has come true. The union between Julian and Alice (of the model) has been determined, but not completely effected. We notice, for example, that Miss Alice in her curtain line uses the future tense, "He will be yours!" (127).

Act III, covering the death of Julian, which follows rapidly his marriage to Miss Alice, contains eight short scenes. In the first, the Butler prepares for departure while Julian cannot understand why everyone has disappeared—even Miss Alice. He feels lost, like a little boy locked in a dark attic closet where no one can hear him and no one is likely to come "for a very long time" (132). The Butler suggests that Miss Alice may be "changing." *Changing* indeed! The word is rich, because in this act she changes in something more than the mere going-away clothes of the newly wed bride. Julian had expected some kind of a wedding reception, to meet her friends; but when he asked her why she had no friends, she had replied, "It is you, Julian, who are being married . . ." (137). Thus, apparently, Miss Alice does not now regard *herself* as married to Julian at all. She has only been the instrument of his marriage to Alice (in the model).

Having accomplished her natural function, she makes plans to depart—where, we know not, but perhaps she goes to repeat a similar kind of plot on other persons of faith—and to leave him to his fate: his ultimate union with Alice (in the model), his lawful bride. But since Alice is an *abstraction*, rather than a real, live person, Julian must first be separated from his own flesh and blood in order, logically speaking, to achieve a more perfect union with Alice. In short, strong metaphysical probability—indeed *necessity*, to use another Aristotelian term—has been properly set up for Julian's death; and he must therefore die.

In the second scene, Miss Alice comes on, dressed in a suit. She sees Julian, says she is sorry, and abruptly leaves. Now more puzzled than ever, Julian asks the Butler if something is being kept from him. The Butler reminds him that he loathes sham, is "dedicated to the reality of things, rather than their appearance" (138). So, when the Butler remarks, "When you are locked in the attic, Julian, in the attic closet, in the dark, do you care who comes?" (139), his words are most significant. This talk about being locked in the closet is, seemingly, a euphemism for dying. Man suffers and he dies, dies alone, the Existentialists tell us. And we see Julian, isolated, reacting with a sense of extreme loneliness at this image of himself (175–76).

The Cardinal arrives in scene three. Julian returns from his premonitory vision of his dying to an assertion of the unspeakable joy his marriage has brought him. As Julian babbles ecstatically about "the blessed wonder of service with a renewing, not an ending joy" (140), that joy he had thought possible only through martyrdom, the Cardinal informs him that the papers will be signed that day. The deal has been completed: "It's all arranged, the grant is accomplished; through your marriage... your service" (141). The Cardinal then gives Julian a word of advice, "As you have accepted what has happened... accept what... *will* happen, *may* happen, with the same humility and .... Accept what may come... as God's will" (142).

Julian begs the Cardinal not to frighten but to bless him. However, the Cardinal's blessing again prepares the audience for the demise of Julian, for he speaks of the "darkness" and prays that Julian may be "worthy of whatever sacrifice, unto death itself" (143). Julian cannot understand this talk about darkness and death because (in his newly married state) everything seems "light" to him. Finally, the Cardinal prays that "the Lord may have mercy on your soul... as, indeed, may He have on us all ... all our souls" (144).

The fourth scene brings the Lawyer on stage. He taunts Julian, comparing him to a Horatio Alger hero, one Frank Fearnought, a "clean-living, healthy farm lad, come from the heartland of the country, from the asylums... in search of fame, and true love—never fortune, of course.... And see what happened to brave and handsome Frank: he has found what he sought... true... love; *and* fortune—to his surprise, for wealth never crossed his pure mind; and fame?... Oooooh, there will be a private fame, perhaps" (145). He also observes that Julian is now dressed in "banker's clothes.... Dressed differently for the *sacrifice, eh?*" (144–45, my italics).

Beyond the Lawyer's ironic ridicule of Julian's ardent desire for service, the actual fact of Julian's having sacrificed himself for the Church, which he supposes will use the immense sum of money as a great power for good in the world, the word *sacrifice*, because of its use in Old Testament and pagan phraseology, functions also as strong preparation for the death of Julian. Julian then goes to look for Miss Alice, leaving the Lawyer and the Cardinal alone in scene five.

The Lawyer now taunts the Cardinal about the large dowry,

the "greatest marriage settlement in history" (146). When the Cardinal points to the model and mysteriously asks if it is really true—what the *it* refers to is anybody's guess (see p. 146)—the Lawyer answers that he doesn't have time to lie to him and that it is. "Can't you accept the wonders of the world? Why not of this one [the model], as well as the other?" he asks the Cardinal (146). Then additional audience preparation for the final incident of Brother Julian's death takes the form of the Lawyer's remarking the distance from the room in which the wedding had occurred to the library, in which they now stand, and saying "we have come quite a . . . *dimension,* have we not?" (147).

It will be recalled that Julian himself had used this same word in referring to his sense of isolation immediately following the wedding (133), as well as in the still earlier incident of the fire in the chapel (94). The word *dimension,* rather than *distance* (which the Cardinal uses), suggests to the audience not only a new development in the plot but also the change from the world of illusion and symbol—the exterior marriage of Julian to Miss Alice—to the world of Platonic reality, the interior wedding of Julian to the abstract Alice of the model.

Immediately after this speech, the Lawyer takes a pistol out of the table drawer, sees that it is in good working order, and tells the Cardinal that they "may have to shoot him [Julian]" (147). He looks at the Cardinal and says: "If the great machinery threatens . . . to come to a halt . . . the great axis on which all turns . . . if it needs oil . . . well, we lubricate it, do we not? And if blood is the only oil handy . . . what is a little blood?" (148).

What is Albee trying to say by this metaphysical image of "the great machinery" and "the great axis"? Is he referring to the machinery of church and court which the Cardinal and Lawyer represent and which frequently oils itself with human blood? Or does he mean that the natural universe itself is oiled with that same sticky lubricant? Either conception is sufficiently surrealistic, and, of course, he could mean both. But our answer to this question affects our definition of Albee's *Weltanschauung* and our own decision as to whether he is speaking solely as a social critic or as a proponent of a kind of Existentialism.

Scene six is very brief. We hear Miss Alice off-stage objecting to appearing before Julian, the Cardinal, and the Lawyer. At the start of scene seven, the Butler, however, pulls her into the

Library (150–85). Miss Alice's reaction to her newly married spouse is very strange; when he asks how she is, she "*moves away from him rather impatiently*" (150). The Cardinal observes that she has changed from her wedding gown, which she explains was "two hundred years old" (150). The Lawyer's laconic comment, "Fragile," applies not only to the wedding gown but also to the marriage, of which it is a symbol, and which was only temporary (150). A silence falls on the group, which eyes Julian "*clinically*" (151) until the Butler pours out some champagne to break the silence. When Miss Alice pledges "the ceremony" (152), Julian does not understand and asks, "What is this about?" and the Lawyer answers "(*Ironic*): When the lights go on all over the world . . . the true world. The ceremony of Alice" (152).

But what is the true world? The suggestion is one stripped of illusion, the abstract one of the model inhabited by tiny Alice. Acting as toastmaster, the Lawyer pledges the various rooms in which the first ceremony had taken place:

> LAWYER: To the chapel wherein they were bound in wedlock. (*A light goes on in a room in the model.* JULIAN *makes sounds of amazement; the others are silent*) To their quarters. (*Light goes on upstairs in the model*) To the private rooms where marriage lives.
>
> BUTLER: To Alice.
>
> MISS ALICES To Alice. (*To which* JULIAN *does not respond this time*).
>
> LAWYER: And to this room . . . (*Another light goes on in the model*) in which they met, in which we are met . . . to celebrate their coming together. (156)

This interesting bit of theater, like the lighting of a Christmas tree, ironically prepares the audience, by way of premonitory illumination, for Julian's own later illumination as to what the world of reality—the world completely stripped of all illusions—is to be like.

A further irony occurs when Julian, "*smiling sweetly,*" and not comprehending what is happening, raises his glass to "the wonders . . . which may befall a man . . . least where he is looking, least that he would have thought; to the clear plan of that which we call *chance,* to what we see as *accident* till our humility returns to us when we are faced with the mysteries" (157, my italics).

Then, to Julian's astonishment, and as in a bad dream, the Lawyer says, "Then, if we're packed, let us go" (157). Julian does not understand that the others are leaving and that he is to be left alone. The Lawyer attempts clarification: "We are leaving you now, Julian; agents, every one of us—going. We are leaving you . . . to your accomplishment: your marriage, your wife, your . . . special priesthood. . . . We go on; you stay" (160–61).

When Julian still refuses to believe, Miss Alice straightens him out, saying, "I have tried to be . . . *her* [Alice]. No; I have tried to be . . . what I thought she might, what might make you happy, what you might use, as a . . . what?" (161). *"Play God,"* interposes the Butler. But Julian had fought doing this all his life: "All my life. In and out of . . . confinement, fought against the symbol" (161–62). "Then you should be happy now," replies Miss Alice. Slowly the horror of what they are demanding he do dawns upon him: "Stay . . . with . . . her?" he asks incredulously (162).

When he remonstrates that he has married *Miss Alice*, not the Alice in the model, Miss Alice kindly rejoins: "No, Julian; you have married *her* . . . through me. . . . You have felt her warmth through me, touched her lips through my lips, held hands, through mine, my breasts, hers, lain on her bed, through mine, wrapped yourself in her wings, your hands on the small of her back, your mouth on her hair, the voice in your ear, hers not mine, all hers; her. You are hers" (163).

They urge him to accept this idea as truth, but he cannot. Rushing to the model, he shouts, "THERE IS NO ONE THERE! . . . THERE IS NOTHING THERE! . . . THERE IS NOTHING THERE!" (164). The Cardinal adds his persuasion to that of the others, for he, too, is ultimately part of the conspiracy against Julian. But to Julian it now seems as if they are asking him to accept as a reality a mere hallucination, for he cannot *see* the figure in the model; and having already fought his way through the asylum period of his life, he does not propose to return to that world of demons. "I HAVE DONE WITH HALLUCINATION," he shouts. To which Miss Alice responds, "Then have done with forgery, Julian; accept what's real. I am the . . . illusion" (167). This speech, perfectly Platonic, is certainly one of the key passages in the entire play.

It comes home to him, finally, that what they are really asking is that he accept as the only reality the hallucinatory world of the model. Julian is deeply confused and agitated by their request, for in his new role as bridegroom Miss Alice is very *real* to him. Yet they are asking him to give her up! Since everything is topsy-turvy, he reasons, perhaps the years he spent in the asylum were years when he was *sane;* therefore he desperately resolves to return there.

Seeing him steadfast in this resolution, the Lawyer forthwith shoots him. Julian "*. . . clutches his belly, stumbles forward a few steps, sinks to the floor in front of the model*" (170). Miss Alice tells the Lawyer that Julian would have stayed, implying that the shooting was unnecessary; but the Lawyer only answers, "It was an accident" (171). The Lawyer refuses to let the Butler call a doctor, and Julian bleeds to death slowly as the Lawyer talks of a sonnet he had written when at school with the Cardinal and of the instructor's comment that the poem had "all the grace of a walking crow" (175). Miss Alice tries to make Julian's last moments as comfortable as possible.

The Lawyer ends his reminiscence with a snide reference to the Cardinal as a "walking bird" and then asks Miss Alice if she is ready to go. Looking up at him with "*sad irony,*" she replies: "Am I ready to go on with it, do you mean? To move to the city now before the train trip south? The private car? The house on the ocean, the . . . same mysteries, the evasions, the perfect plotting? The removed residence, the Rolls twice weekly in to the shopping strip . . . all of it?" (177).

We gather from this speech that the same tragedy may be enacted many more times in the future by these same three plotters, these same agents of fate, although with different victims (160). Unlike the end of Beckett's *Waiting for Godot,* which is appropriately static after dramatizing the experience of continually frustrated expectation, the ending of Albee's *Tiny Alice* implies a kind of eternal cycle in which men of faith are sacrificed on the altar as an offering to whatever grim forces in the universe preside over their ultimate destinies. The game goes on, as the Lawyer explains, "until we are replaced," the "we" referring to himself, the Butler, and Miss Alice. "Or," he adds, "until everything is desert . . . on the chance that *it* runs out before *we* do" (178). Here, as earlier, Albee has one of his characters offer a view of the universe as a dying entity.

As an agent in this cosmic drama, Miss Alice, portraying illusion, must have her stage dress in order. She therefore asks the Butler to get her wig, which she had first used to present herself as an old lady to Julian. He answers testily that he is busy covering the furniture with sheets. The Lawyer gets her the wig, but then playfully puts it on the bust of the phrenological head that sits on the library table (23, 183), thereby symbolizing that Julian has been hoodwinked (as so many before him?) by illusion. "Looks nice there," the Lawyer says of the wig. "Leave it," he says to Miss Alice, "we'll get you another" (183). For the fooling of their next victim, presumably!

Then, as Julian, feeling that he has been abandoned by his God, intones the thirteenth psalm, "How long wilt thou forget me, O Lord? Forever? . . . How long wilt thou hide thy face from me? . . . How long shall my enemy be exalted over me?" (180), all three leave him; and their departure is highly ritualistic. We note, for example, that Julian dismisses Miss Alice with an angry tone. If nothing else, he has at least learned that she, in her role of Illusion, has betrayed him; and he wants nothing more to do with her or her sympathy. The Luciferesque Lawyer walks over to where Julian is lying propped up against the model, a pose that he finds richly ironic because of Julian's refusal to accept the superficial god of other men, the world of illusion that Miss Alice epitomizes, and bids him "*almost casually*" "Goodbye" (185). Julian curses him as the devil, calling him "Instrument!"

The last to leave, the Butler, having covered everything and having put everything in so-called order, dutifully bids Julian farewell, kissing him on the forehead—the stage directions call for "*not a quick kiss*"—and saying, "Goodbye, dear Julian," as he exits and closes the doors behind him (185).

It is literally the kiss of death that the Butler implants on Julian's brow, and the last scene of the play (scene eight) presents Julian's protracted dying in such a way as to involve the entire audience. At its climax the play transforms itself, therefore, into a deeply moving ceremony in which the members of the audience experience with Brother Julian the fear and pity of dying.

In approaching the manifold difficulties of interpreting this final scene, I find that the best plan seems to be, first, to present a short analysis of Julian's state of mind during the long soliloquy that makes up this scene (186–90) and, second, to describe the effect of the spectacular devices that emphasize the audience participation in the solemn rite of Julian's heroic demise.

What passes through Julian's mind, first and foremost, is his sudden abandonment by the woman he had so recently married. He soliloquizes as if the other three characters are near the door, listening to what he has to say. Second, he finds it hard to comprehend that he really is dying. Loudly he says, "I HAVE NEVER DREAMED OF IT. NEVER . . . IMAGINED. . ." (186) what dying would be like. Nevertheless he says that he "died once" (figuratively) when he was "little." And, third, he now reminisces about a boyhood accident, which closely parallels his present plight.

By alternating Julian's inner thought with these loud appeals to the other three characters and to God (who, he thinks, has also forsaken him), Albee achieves considerable variety in this long, dramatic soliloquy. Only a very skillful actor (such as Sir John Gielgud) could possibly sustain it to an effective climax.

Besides these three elements of the soliloquy, there is a fourth, and even more important, one—his address to Alice in the model. She, too, he thinks, has forsaken him. "*Hast* thou forsaken me . . . with . . . all the others?" (187), he asks, laughing at and mocking himself as the groom of the tiny Alice in the model, as though he were only a play-priest working in a dollhouse: " 'Raise high the roofbeam, for the bridegroom comes.' Oh, what a priesthood is this! Oh, what a range of duties, and such parishioners, and such a chapel for my praise. (*Turns some, leans toward the model, where the chapel light shines*) Oh, what a priesthood, see my chapel, how it . . ." (188).

Shines, he was about to say. But "*Suddenly the light in the chapel in the model goes out. JULIAN starts, makes a sound of surprise and fear*" (188). At the same time, the dim sounds of a magnified heartbeat and of labored breathing become audible to the audience. Since Julian does not yet hear this sound, he continues his ironical mocking of himself, this time noticing the phrenological head bedecked with Miss Alice's wig, which he crawls toward and half-kneels in front of, asking,

> Thou art my bride? Thou? For thee have I done my life? Grown to love, entered in, bent . . . accepted? For thee?

> Is that the . . . awful humor? Art thou the true arms, when the warm flesh [of Miss Alice] I touched . . . rested against, was . . . nothing? And *she* . . . was not real? Is thy stare the true look? Unblinking, outward, through, to some horizon? And her eyes . . . warm, accepting, were they . . . not real? Art thou my bride? . . . Ah God! Is that the humor? THE ABSTRACT? . . . REAL? THE REST . . . FALSE? (*To himself, with terrible irony*) It is what I have wanted, have insisted on. Have nagged . . . for. (*Looking about the room, raging*) IS THIS MY PRIESTHOOD, THEN? THIS WORLD? [of the model and of the cold statue]. (188–89)

If this be so, he hurls defiance at the universe, like Ahab in pursuit of Moby Dick, and shouts, "THEN COME AND SHOW THYSELF! BRIDE? GOD?" (189).

As if in answer to his challenge comes the sound of the heartbeats and breathing. "SHOW THYSELF! I DEMAND THEE!" He shouts at the model. "SHOW THYSELF! FOR THEE I HAVE GAMBLED . . . MY SOUL? I DEMAND THY PRESENCE. ALICE!" (189). Again, in answer to his defiance, the physiological sounds now become louder; moreover, at the same time, the light fades in the bedroom of the model and "*begins to move across the upper story,*" a cue which Julian reacts to with "*a muffled cry*" (189). As he appeals to the mercy of God, the "*lights keep moving* [ever closer]," and the sounds become terrifyingly louder. Now they fill the entire theater, and the captive audience is also terrified by them, as in an awful nightmare. Nevertheless there is no letup in the crescendo of the sounds, which become "*enormous,*" "*deafening,*" as a great shadow fills and darkens the entire stage, "*the shadow of a great presence,*" a shadow that engulfs Julian (189–90).

III *Man and Illusion*

This presence, I take it, is paradoxically that of *tiny* Alice herself, the purified abstraction, the only reality, the God Julian has believed in—the reality of death. This fourfold equation of death and reality as well as of, concurrently, God and Alice—along with the very explicit stage direction that Julian is to die with arms outstretched in the manner of "*a crucifixion*"—may suggest that the terrible and unbearable reality men are really never prepared to face is their own death, and that to circumlocute it in their thinking they generally build a world of illusion. Accordingly, all men ultimately share a somewhat similar fate, even those who are not so honest in their thinking as Julian was; for all men suffer and die. In a sense we are all "crucified." Julian heroically accepts this knowledge with resignation at the moment of his death. Bravely facing these fundamental realities of human existence and its erasure while at the same time clinging to his faith, Julian may thus typify the Existentialist hero as believer.

Consequently the play, according to this reading, would still be something more than one more comment on the by now well-worn theme that man cannot live without illusions, such as we find in O'Neill's *The Iceman Cometh* and in Gorky's earlier *The Lower Depths.* Thus construed, *Tiny Alice* is a rite of death, with a certain sublimity of theatricality which, when properly presented, should move an audience to tears.[13] And the evocation of a god, tiny Alice—her shadow, her actual appearance on the stage (as in the previously mentioned *wayang* plays)—may show something of the dramatist's purpose.

That objective might be defined as an attempt to dramatize an unvarnished Reality, one entirely free of any artificiality, falsehood, or illusion—literally to parade it upon a stage not used to seeing it there. In this sense, the appearance of the great shadow would amount to an enormous triumph not only for Julian's faith in his own special God but also for Albee's desire to reform the theater. It is really a pity that Artaud could not have lived to see this play, for it embodies so many of his theories concerning new theater.

CHAPTER *10*

The Well-Made Play in the Theater of the Absurd

I *The Structure*

UNIFIED IN ACTION, time, and place, *A Delicate Balance* is in some ways the nearest thing to a traditional well-made play of Scribe or Sardou that Albee has ever composed. It recalls their suspenseful and cleverly constructed plots, but it exhibits a greater depth of characterization than their plays do. The whole Albee play takes place in one set—the combination library-living room of "a large and well-appointed suburban house."[1] The action—about a married couple (Harry and Edna) who try to move into the household of another couple (Tobias and Agnes) at the same time that the latter couple's daughter returns home—spans barely more than twenty-four hours, from Friday night to early Sunday morning.

The context of the play specifies "autumn" as the season (4, 40), an appropriate tonal designation for the time of life of the principal actors (both couples are in their fifties), as well as for the situation of *drift* in which they find themselves. In the first scene Agnes speaks to her husband, Tobias, of her belief that she might lose her mind and of her being surprised by the "lack of unpleasantness" which is associated with this belief (10). Also in this first scene, Agnes' alcoholic sister Claire, who is staying with them and who is "*several years younger*," is talked about; and we learn of Tobias' liking for her as he defends her to his wife (7, 11). Their daughter Julia is mentioned, too (12). The situation of the play, as Agnes propounds it to Tobias, is as follows: "You have hope, only, of growing even older than you are in the company of your steady wife, your alcoholic sister-in-law and occasional visits . . . from our melancholy Julia" (12).

Claire comes on stage in scene two, apologizing for having earlier that evening, apparently, caused a disturbance at dinner. When Agnes asks what she apologizes for, Claire answers: "I apologize that my nature is such [as] to bring out in you the full force of your brutality" (13). Agnes, in the act of leaving to phone her daughter Julia, says to Claire:

> *If* you come to the dinner table unsteady, *if* when you try to say good evening and weren't the autumn colors lovely today you are nothing but vowels, and *if* one smells the vodka on you from across the room—and *don't* tell me again, *either* of you! that vodka leaves nothing on the breath: if you are expecting it, if you are sadly and wearily expecting it, it *does—if* these conditions exist . . . *persist* . . . then the reaction of one who is burdened by her love is not brutality—though it would be excused, believe me! —not brutality at all, but the souring side of love. (13)

Left alone, in scene three (14–26), Tobias and Claire with playful sophistication consider killing Agnes, a suggestion first made by Claire. They also talk about Claire's alcoholism and about Tobias' friendship with Harry. "What do you have in common with your very best friend?" she asks, " 'cept the coincidence of having cheated on your wives in the same summer with the same woman . . . girl . . . woman? What except that? And hardly a distinction. I believe she was upended that whole July" (19–20). She pursues this question of friendship between the two men: "Would you give Harry the shirt off your back, as they say?"; and Tobias answers: "I *suppose* I would. He *is* my best friend" (21). According to Claire, a friend is "to listen to Bruckner with . . . to tell you're sick of golf . . . to admit to that—now and then—you're suddenly frightened and you don't know why" (21).

Then primed with a cigarette and a glass of brandy and lying on the floor, she casually invites him to make love to her (22). And from this same position on the floor she tells him of her one and only unsuccessful attempt to overcome her weakness with the help of Alcoholics Anonymous. This scene, quite long and important, shows the relationship between Tobias and Claire to be something more than that of mere brother-in-law and sister-in-law.

Agnes returns on stage, marking scene four, after having talked with Julia and discovering that she is coming home *again*

—from her fourth husband, Douglas (30). "Right on schedule, once every three years," quips Claire (31). Besides providing this announcement, this scene develops the battle between the two sisters. When Agnes wants Tobias to talk to Claire, he reminisces instead about a cat which had stopped liking him and which he in frustration had had killed. The elaboration of this story (34–37), which grows out of the previous talk about friendship and love, serves to symbolize Tobias' feeling about his marriage with Agnes. Tobias feels guilty about having had his cat killed by a veterinarian; and when he babbles on to himself, Claire interrupts: "Oh, stop it! 'Love' is not the problem. You love Agnes and Agnes loves Julia and Julia loves me and I love you. We all love each other; yes we do. We love each other" (37). This talk is interrupted by the arrival of a car in their driveway.

If the announcement, in scene four, of Julia's return home after her fourth unsuccessful marriage begins the complication of the triangle situation of Tobias, Agnes, and Claire, the arrival of Tobias' friend Harry and Edna, his wife, in scene five completes it. When Harry and Edna try to make conversation, Claire asks them why they have come: "We were . . . sitting home . . . just sitting home. . . . ," Harry begins to explain, amid various conversational interruptions; and he repeats this same phrase three times (41–44). Edna was working on her needle point, and he was reading his French; and then—had come the fear: "I . . . I don't know quite what happened then; we . . . we were . . . it was all very quiet, and we were all alone. . . . We got scared. . . . It was like being lost: very young again, with the dark, and lost. There was no . . . thing . . . to be . . . frightened of, but. . . . We couldn't stay there, and so we came here. You're our very best friends" (45–47).

This speech of Harry's is delivered with various accompaniments from Edna, including her tears, sobbing and "*quiet hysteria*" (47). Harry concludes, "We can't go back there." Then, after other appeals in the name of friendship, Harry and Edna are led by Agnes to Julia's vacant room. "I was wondering when it [the trouble] would begin . . . when it would start," remarks Claire to Tobias (49)—her comment and dramatic function reminiscent of a *ficelle* in a Henry James story.

As a whole, the function of Act I is to introduce the characters—all of them except Julia appear on stage; and even she is talked about. More important, however, the act introduces a twofold complication to our triangle—Julia's falling out with her fourth husband and Harry and Edna's moving in.

Act II, Albee has divided into two large divisions or "Scenes." The first of these occurs before dinner on the next evening (Saturday); the second, after dinner. The first division contains five scenes. In the first of these, Julia, now arrived, complains to her mother about finding Harry and Edna in her room; and Agnes tells her why they are there. We also learn that the visiting couple has remained in this room all day (55). Agnes bemoans her lot as a woman, wishing she had been born a man and talking about reversals of the sexes, which makes Julia angry because she wants to talk about the disruption of her own marriage. She tells her mother to "go straight to hell" (58).

Tobias comes on as Agnes marches off; and Julia forthwith quarrels with him not only because of the Harry-and-Edna presence but also because she thinks him insufficiently sympathetic to her marital situation. He, on the other hand, is plagued by a combination of factors—the Harry-and-Edna presence, the female jealousy and fighting between Claire and his wife, the government investigation of his income tax, and Julia's return home. As he says, "This isn't the first time, you know. This isn't the first time you've come back with one of your goddamned marriages on the rocks. Four! Count 'em!" (62). To her, he is no longer "marvel—saint, sage, daddy, everything," that he was during her "somewhat angular adolescence" (63). Nor is he any longer even the "very nice but ineffectual, essential, but not-really-thought-of, gray . . . non-eminence" that he had become for her at a later period (63–64). Now, to her, he is nothing but "nasty, violent, absolutely human man!" (64). He offers to speak to Doug, her fourth, but she thinks it will do no good.

In the next scene, the third, Claire comes in, greets Julia warmly, asks for a drink, and tells of her adventure of the day —a humorous account of her unsuccessful attempt to buy a topless (or bottomless) bathing suit. But, beneath the playful mask of her clowning, we detect her deep frustration, particularly when she pleads with Tobias to take both Julia and herself away "to where it is always good and happy" (70). "Would you, Dad?" Julia asks solicitously. But Tobias only frowns and says, "It's . . . it's too late, or something" (70).

After more talk of Julia's marital problems and characterization of Claire as a sideline sitter and "objective observer" (70), Agnes comes in with the latest report on Harry and Edna: "I *happened* upstairs, and I knocked at Harry and Edna's *Julia's* room, door, and after a moment I heard Harry say, 'It's all right; we're all right.'... I am told—*they* tell me that while we were all out... Edna descended, asked them to make sandwiches, which were brought to the closed door and handed in.... There is no point in pressing it, they are our very dear friends, they will tell us in good time" (73). Then Julia reverts to talk about her husband, Doug, who she claims is opposed to "EVERYTHING!" (76); and she waxes emotional until Tobias shouts for her to be still.

In the fifth scene Harry and Edna appear in the doorway with their coats. They are leaving—but will be back after dinner. After they go, Julia, "*near tears,*" says with great intensity, "I want my room back! I want my room back!" Dinner is announced as the curtain comes down on this first division of Act II.

The second division—what Albee calls "scene two" (79–119)—embraces ten shorter scenes. The first of the ten scenes defines the character of Agnes as the fulcrum in the delicately balanced family, despite the fact that Julia calls her more of "a drill sergeant!" (80, 81–83). In the second, Claire comes in and clowns with an accordion, blasting out chords to punctuate high points in the dialogue. She continues her fight with Agnes, carrying it so far as to inform Julia of her own and her mother's premarital sexual encounters (85). Meanwhile, Tobias is being needled by Agnes for his inaction. She and he finally move off, together, to "do something" (84, 91).

After they are gone, Julia propounds in scene three *the* question: "Harry and Edna: what do they want?" "Succor," replies Claire; "Comfort.... Warmth. A special room with a night light, or the door ajar so you can look down the hall from the bed and see that Mommy's door is open." "But that's my room," responds Julia. Claire answers, "It's... the *room.* Happens you *were* in it. You're a visitor as much as anyone, *now*" (First italics, Albee's; last two, mine.) [91–92].

In scene four, Edna returns and announces that she and Harry are back. Julia, angered by Claire's quips about her marriages, vents her wrath on Edna, who is her godmother. In the fifth scene Harry comes in and is about to fix himself a drink; but

Julia rushes to the bar, throws herself protectingly across it as if it were a family altar about to be desecrated, and strenuously appeals all the while to her parents for assistance. Receiving no help from Agnes, who is present, she becomes distraught and runs wildly from the room, calling for her father.

Remarking that "that's the first time she's called on her father in . . . since her childhood," Agnes then reminisces in scene six about how Julia, as a child, had reacted to the death of her brother Teddy—a reminiscence that leads to memory of her own state of mind at that time. "It was an unreal time," she says. "I thought Tobias was out of love with me—or, rather, was tired of it, when Teddy died, as if that had been the string" (101). She continues:

> Ah, the things I doubted then: that I was loved—that *I* loved—that Teddy had ever lived at all. . . . That Julia would be with us long. . . . I thought Tobias was unfaithful to me then. Was he, Harry?
>
> EDNA: Oh, Agnes.
>
> HARRY (*Unsubtle*): Come on, Agnes! Of course not! No!
>
> AGNES (*Faint amusement*): Was he, Claire? That hot summer, with Julia's knees all bloody and Teddy dead? Did my husband . . . cheat on me?
>
> CLAIRE (*Looks at her steadily, toasts her; then*): Ya got me, Sis. (102)

Then, turning a cold, precise, and not-too-nice gaze on Harry and Edna, Agnes asks them, "What do you want? . . . What do you *really* . . . *want?*" Her pressing of this question arouses Edna's anger, which is smoothed over by Claire's offering to yodel and accompany herself on the accordion.

Tobias appears in scene seven to demand why Julia is upstairs "in hysterics" (106). His vivid description of her prepares for the next scene (the eighth) in which Julia appears, her hair wild, "her face . . . tear-streaked," and threatens Harry and Edna with Tobias' pistol. Tobias talks her into giving it up to him. But when she asks Harry and Edna if they mean to stay *forever*, Edna replies:

> If need be . . . we come where the table has been laid for us in such an event . . . where the bed is turned down . . . and

warmed . .. and has been ready should we need it. . . .
AGNES: You have come to live with us, then. . . .
EDNA: Why, yes; we have. (116–17)

Thus, like Poe's raven, Harry and Edna become symbols; they represent the inevitable march of spiritual aridity into the most sacred oasis in the modern wasteland—the home. The invasion of this stronghold of privacy drives Julia to near madness; helpless as a child, she is led off at the end of this scene by Agnes. In the two remaining very brief scenes Harry and Edna say good night and go upstairs to bed; Tobias, after saying a firm good night to Claire, decides to sit up the rest of the night.

Act II has its action clearly focused around Julia, who not only initiates the action (the unsuccessful attempt at getting rid of Harry and Edna) but also keeps it moving to its crisis at the end of the act. At that point, however, Tobias remains alone on the stage, hinting at the transfer to him of responsibility for the final action.

Consequently, we see Tobias in Act II as the principal center of the struggle, as the agent finally responsible for bringing about the resolution. The first long scene indicates little progress, however, toward such a resolution (121–34). It is seven-thirty on Sunday morning; and the others are not yet up, when Agnes and Tobias converse gently about the events of the previous night—the past, her suspicions of Claire, and so on. But when she asks him "What did you decide?" he has to admit that, despite having stayed up all night, he is no nearer to having solved the Harry-and-Edna problem than before (128, 130, 133).

Julia comes in (scene two), apologizes for her hysterical conduct of the previous night, and then goes off to make coffee. Left alone, Agnes and Tobias continue their talk—ranging over the relationships of husbands and wives, Agnes' disappointment at the breakup of Julia's fourth marriage and at her own frustrated hopes for a grandchild, the death of their son Teddy, and her feeling that Tobias had not wanted another child. When he finally asks, "What are we going to do? About everything?" (139), she answers that they will do whatever he likes.

When Claire bounces in, she is sent to the kitchen to help Julia with the coffee. Tobias finally blurts out, "Shall I ask them to leave?" "Who?" asks Agnes (140).

TOBIAS (*Defiant*): Harry and Edna?
AGNES (*Tiny laugh*): Oh. For a moment I thought you meant Julia and Claire.

....

TOBIAS (*Anger rising*): . . . why *don't* I throw Julia and Claire out instead? Or better yet, why don't I throw the whole bunch out!? *[sic]*
AGNES: Or get rid of me! That would be easier: rid yourself of the harridan. Then you can run your mission and take out sainthood papers. (141)

Faced with these four possibilities, Tobias cannot decide what to do.

When Julia and Claire return with coffee, matters don't improve. For Julia angers Claire by suggesting that she have some vodka in her orange juice, and Claire retaliates by calmly pouring Julia's orange juice on the rug. Looking at the mess Claire has made on the rug, Julia shrugs her shoulders and says, "Well, why not. Nothing changes" (146). This action brings Tobias to his feet as he tries to restore order in the family he ostensibly heads. As he explains to them, he has been thinking, all night long, about the problem; but now he finds Julia as his opponent. "HARRY AND EDNA ARE OUR FRIENDS!!" he shouts at her with frustration and rage. "THEY ARE INTRUDERS!!" she shouts back in precisely the same tone (149). And this interchange defines the conflict.

After Claire comments on the way each person is reacting to this crisis, singling out Agnes' silence in the face of her usual role as a person characteristically "talky" and inclined to be "ruler of the roost" (149), Agnes says that she, too, has "been thinking about Harry and Edna; about disease" (150); and she proceeds to develop the Harry-Edna visitation into an image of "the plague." "They've brought the plague with them," she explains. "It is not Edna and Harry who have come to us—our friends—it is a disease" (151).

Then the talk turns to how they should meet this plague. Is anyone of them immune? Claire claims that she has "had it" and is still alive (152). Agnes, however, coolly considers the lack of immunity of the others and says, "If we're not . . . well, why not be infected, why not die of it? We're bound to die of something

. . . soon, or in a while. Or shall we burn them out, rid ourselves of it all . . . and wait for the next invasion." And then, turning to Tobias, she adds, "You decide, my darling." At this suspenseful moment Harry and Edna suddenly appear in the room—dressed, *"but not with coats"* (152).

The scene that follows is undoubtedly the most important in the entire play. Edna announces that Harry wants to talk to Tobias; and the three women, highly alert to this long-awaited cue, move off to the kitchen with Edna to "make a proper breakfast" (153). After they have gone, Harry and Tobias stall considerably, but finally prime themselves with drinks and get down to business:

> TOBIAS: . . . By God, it isn't easy, Harry . . . but we can make it . . . if you want us to . . . *I* can, I mean, I *think* I can.
> HARRY: No . . . we're . . . we're going, Tobias.
> TOBIAS: I don't know what help . . . I don't know *how* . . .
> HARRY: I said: we're *going*.
> TOBIAS: Yes, but . . . you're going?
> HARRY (*Nice, shy smile*): Sure.
> TOBIAS: . . . . You can't go back there; you've got to. . . .
> HARRY: Got to what? Sell the house? Buy another? Move to the club? (157–58)

Then, in the manner of a duet, Harry asks, three times, "Do you *want* us here, Tobias?" Each time Tobias can only exclaim incoherently, with a variety of stress on his last two words, "You came *here!*" (158). Harry says that he had talked their visit over with Edna; if Tobias and Agnes had come to them, they (Harry and Edna) would not have taken them in; and he concludes: "You . . . you don't *want* us, do you, Toby? You don't want us here" (159).

Albee offers the following direction for the next long soliloquy of Tobias (159–62): *"This next is an aria. It must have in its performance all the horror and exuberance of a man who has kept his emotions under control too long.* TOBIAS *will be carried to the edge of hysteria, and he will find himself laughing, sometimes, while he cries from sheer release. All in all, it is genuine and bravura at the same time, one prolonging the other"* (159).

The soliloquy begins with bitter irony, shouted; and it ends with tears and soft talk:

> YES! OF COURSE! I WANT YOU HERE! I HAVE BUILT THIS HOUSE! I WANT YOU IN IT! I WANT YOUR PLAGUE! YOU'VE GOT SOME TERROR WITH YOU? BRING IT IN! . . . .
>
> You come for dinner don't you come for cocktails see us at the club on Saturdays and talk and lie and laugh with us and pat old Agnes on the hand and say you don't know what old Toby'd do without her and we've known you all these years and we love each other don't we? . . . . So, bring your wife, and bring your terror, bring your plague. (*Loud*) BRING YOUR PLAGUE! (*The four women appear in the archway, coffee cups in hand, stand, watch*) I DON'T WANT YOU HERE! YOU ASKED! NO! I DON'T (*Loud*) BUT BY CHRIST YOU'RE GOING TO STAY HERE! . . . . DO YOU HEAR ME?! YOU BRING YOUR TERROR AND YOU COME IN HERE AND YOU LIVE WITH US! YOU BRING YOUR PLAGUE! YOU STAY WITH US! I DON'T WANT YOU HERE! I DON'T LOVE YOU! BUT BY GOD . . . YOU STAY!! (*Pause*) STAY! (*Softer*) Stay! (*Soft, tears*) Stay, please? Stay? (*Pause*) Stay? Please? Stay? (160–62)

The last two scenes wrap up the play. In the first of these, Edna and Harry say a prolonged good-by (163–68); in the second, we see the family after they have gone. In the first, Agnes philosophizes vaguely in a manner reminiscent of T. S. Eliot about time, continuing some of the earlier Existential echoes of the play (152): "Time happens, I suppose. . . . To people. Everything becomes . . . too late, finally. You know it's going on . . . up on the hill; you can see the dust, and hear the cries, and the steel . . . but you wait; and time happens. When you *do* go, sword, shield . . . finally . . . there's nothing there . . . save rust; bones; and the wind" (164).

When Edna invites Agnes to go into town with her "on Thursday," she declines, saying she has "so much to do" (166). Albee also gives the curtain speech to Agnes; and considering her role as preserver of the "delicate balance," doing so is appropriate:

> What I find most astonishing—aside from my belief that I will, one day . . . lose my mind . . . or that I'll not *know* if it happens, or maybe even *has*—what I find most astonishing, I think, is the wonder of daylight, of the sun. All the centuries, millenniums—all the history—I wonder if that's why we sleep at night, because the darkness still . . . frightens us? They say we sleep to let the demons out—to let the mind go raving mad, our dreams and nightmares all our logic gone awry, the dark side of our reason. And when the daylight comes again . . . comes order with it. (*Sad*

chuckle) Poor Edna and Harry. (*Sigh*) Well, they're safely gone ... and we'll all forget ... quite soon. (*Pause*) Come now; we can begin the day. (170)

A Delicate Balance won the Pulizer Prize for drama in 1967, and the play marked nearly a decade of Albee's prominence in the American theater.

CHAPTER *11*

Albee's Place in the Theater

THE RESPONSE of critics to Albee's plays is voluminous enough to constitute a book in itself, but we can only indicate a few main points about each play because of space limitations.

The Zoo Story received more good reviews than bad ones. Harold Clurman found it the most interesting play of the season, and Henry Hewes and George Wellwarth also praised the arrival of Albee as a young playwright of great promise.[1] The play engendered controversy about its theme; some critics mistakenly attacked the action as improbable and the ending as melodramatic; and still others (Wellwarth and Brustein) made unfounded remarks about the character of Jerry.[2] The dialogue, however, was praised; and the play as a whole was compared advantageously with its companion piece, Samuel Beckett's *Krapp's Last Tape.*[3]

Some of the critics—Paul Cubeta for one—raised some interesting questions about satire and symbolism in *The Sandbox*, particularly in connection with its theme—the experience of dying.[4] But his statement that the play purposed "to explore the deeper implications of a world in which man is out of harmony with himself, his fellowman, and his environment" missed the rich particularity which makes the play so admirable a work of art.[5] Other critics also misstated the theme, overstressing the importance of dialogue and neglecting the action while making misleading or caviling remarks about characterization.[6] Wellwarth unfairly dismissed this play as a mere sketch preliminary to *The American Dream*, but Richard Watts and Walter Kerr praised it as "a chilling surrealist gem" and as "a soft little elegy."[7] Generally speaking, the play was well received and successful.

The Death of Bessie Smith encountered much, although qualified, critical opposition. Meaning and plot were objected to as unclear; tone and music were labeled *inappropriate;* but the dialogue was praised as "superbly spiky."[8] Tom Prideaux called it Albee's "least successful play" because it had symbols instead of real live people for characters; James Baldwin objected to the "bloodless" portrait of Bessie Smith.[9] The critics generally approved of the theme as an important one for a young playwright to handle, but they also thought something in the characterization had misfired.[10]

Critical response to *The American Dream* was mainly favorable. The critics made much—too much, in my opinion—of its similarity in matter and technique to Ionesco's *The Bald Soprano.* Other writers—Ibsen, Strindberg, Chekhov, Kafka, Gertrude Stein —were also cited as possible sources or influences.[11] Many critical statements overemphasized horror, homosexuality, and the zany quality of the dialogue.[12] One critic thought the set "all wrong," but Whitney Balliett and Clurman praised it highly.[13]

The notorious success of *Who's Afraid of Virginia Woolf?* can be summarized under four main headings: general emotional effect on the audience; controversies over interpretation; criticisms of plot, characters, and dialogue; and comparisons with other playwrights. Some of the critics attacked the audience for complicity with the actors to achieve "a mock catharsis."[14] Emil Roy offered an extended Jungian analysis in terms of symbols.[15] Diana Trilling worried herself into thinking the play a "contemporary allegory" of the atom bomb, although she admitted that the author had given "no such account of his play."[16] She objected all the while to the fact that the public was receiving the play not as an allegory but as a transcript of real life, and she asserted that the characters were not true to "American academic life."[17] For most of the critics, the play was too long, the business of the imaginary child was unconvincing, and the diction too dirty.[18] Many of the critical statements took, as usual, the form of comparisons with other writers (Americans this time)—O'Neill, Tennessee Williams, Lillian Hellman, Jack London—but also with many non-Americans from Euripides to Strindberg, Ibsen, and Genet.[19]

Despite the fact *The Ballad of the Sad Cafe* was regarded as an unusually faithful adaptation of Carson McCullers' novella, it received only "mixed" reviews; Albee's use of Southern dialect was attacked as unconvincing. *Malcolm*, another of Albee's adaptations, failed utterly, mainly because of bad writing, according to a consensus of critics.[20] Previously his adaptation of Melville's *Bartleby, the Scrivener* had failed. And, currently, his adaptation of Giles Cooper's *Everything in the Garden* has met stiff criticism. (See *supra.*)

Tiny Alice, probably more than any other Albee play, was subjected to a confusion of interpretation by the critics, who refused to accept it on its own surrealistic terms. Although the theatrical appeal of the play was praised, its metaphysical quality was censured as unclear.[21]

Clurman and Brustein represent extremes of the respectively sympathetic and unsympathetic reaction to *A Delicate Balance;* both critics regarded dialogue as the point at issue in the success or failure of this play.[22] More than in *Tiny Alice*, the hand of T. S. Eliot (in works like *The Cocktail Party* and *The Family Reunion*) appeared clearly visible to several critics.[23] Others saw situational resemblances to such plays as Pinter's *The Room* and *The Caretaker*, while a few made much of the point that Albee had borrowed from himself—particularly, they noted that the tale of the cat in *A Delicate Balance* resembled that of Jerry and the dog in *The Zoo Story*, and the dead-child motif in *Balance* reminded them of the imaginary-son business in *Virginia Woolf* and the dismembered son in *The American Dream.*[24]

After almost a decade of Edward Albee's plays, it should be possible to make some kind of fair assessment of his work. At the moment, he is the American leader in the "theater of the absurd," the most promising and controversial experimental movement that has occurred for many a day in the American theater. But, although Albee's reputation is international, we would certainly not think of rating him as highly as Eugene O'Neill. O'Neill won the Nobel Prize after a long and arduous struggle, being cited as the first American dramatist to achieve widespread recognition on the Continental stage. Albee, on the other hand, attained international fame, although less distinguished than O'Neill's, with relative ease—overnight, as it were —with the production of *The Zoo Story* in Berlin, American producers having been unwilling to gamble on his work up to that time.

The comparison with O'Neill may not be entirely farfetched, for Albee has won a name for himself as an experimenter; and his new plays are awaited always with anticipation of something strange, fascinating, exciting, or alarming—much as were the works of O'Neill during the 1920's, although O'Neill seemingly encountered less hostility from his audience and his critics than has Albee.

The appearance of more and more of Albee's plays in anthologies of modern drama and even in some rather conservative ones surveying all of American literature would certainly indicate some rather pronounced degree of acceptance, however begrudgingly bestowed. Furthermore, Albee has won more critical attention—possibly because many critics regard him as a dangerous influence—than perhaps any other American writer for the stage in an equal period of years. There seems no denying that he is an "established" writer today, particularly as he continues creating new plays and seems to possess the capacity to accept his failures in his stride. No one can doubt the seriousness with which he takes himself in his career as playwright.

As a writer, Edward Albee brings to the American stage an extreme lack of sentimentality, one that in many cases his audience may not be prepared for. Often this quality shows itself in his diction and in his dialogue: his "merciless ear for [exposing] the clichés, *non sequiturs* and droning repetitions of everyday talk."[25] Yet, with the possible exception of *The American Dream*, he has not really been an effective *satirist;* for he seems, in his plays, to lack belief that correction is possible. And so we are left with a feeling of absurdity and despair that can hardly be classified as a remedy for social evils. More than one critic has leveled against him the charge that he lacks *any* set of values with which to make events morally significant; and perhaps this quality, for some, makes his serious attempts at tragedy sometimes fall so flat.

At the same time, Albee certainly has the power to produce powerful emotional effects, as his better work in *Virginia Woolf*, *Tiny Alice*, and even *A Delicate Balance* clearly shows. Moreover, he knows the theater well. As one writer states, "It would be shameful cowardice to deny that he [Albee] is the possessor of rare gifts for dramatic writing. . . ."[26] Yet, despite this widely acknowledged literary gift—despite his honesty and skill—he has certainly not turned out to be "the mid-century Elijah"[27] for whom some had hoped—nor, for that matter, a modern Euripides. He resists classification, therefore, as either a tragedian or a social critic.

Although it is customary to grant an author his *donnée,* his starting point with regard to his subject matter, Albee has probably encountered more opposition in this one area than any other young writer today. One critic has broadly defined Albee's themes as "the destruction of children by parents, and of men and women by each other."[28] Another has chided him for not pursuing "larger, more universal themes," particularly as this writer thinks the American public is ready for them.[29] But anyone who "unmasks the monstrous in our ordinary selves"[30] is not likely to be popular with a non-self-critical audience such as one sometimes meets in our theater.

Currently, Albee is reported to be at work in Paris on two short one-act plays—"Seascape" and "All Over"—with a collective title of "Life and Death."[31] This title would certainly seem to indicate a broad enough theme. At the same time, he has said in various interviews that he is also prospecting a full-length play to be called "The Substitute Speaker," which, according to Henry Hewes, will treat Albee's prevalent theme—frequently stated by Albee himself in the form of a question—" 'How much reality are human beings equipped to face?' "[32]

Historically considered, Albee falls directly in the long line of the French theater extending back as far as the *fin-de-siècle* Surrealism of Alfred Jarry's *Ubu Roi.* But, on the American scene, Albee's strangely fascinating experiments, his adaptation of what the French call "black humor" to American settings, are akin to the revolution in poetry that occurred in the early 1920's when Pound, Eliot, and others looked backward to the English metaphysical poets of the seventeenth century and saw in them a possibility for a new kind of modern poetry by shaping their methods to new subject matter.

One of the big questions, I suppose, in evaluating the place of Albee in the modern theater, is whether or not the phenomenon characterized as "theater of the absurd" will last. As one writer observes, "In the arts the new becomes old with merciless speed, and these new playwrights already seem in need of something new to say. At their best, however, they have given theatrical expression to the spiritual fallout which has been as much a reality as the physical fallout in their imperiled times."[33]

It will be interesting, therefore, to observe whether or not Albee, who is still relatively young, can continue his present leading position in the theater, one which some critics have accounted for by the dearth of good writers and good plays. Certainly Tennessee Williams' statement that "Edward Albee is the only great playwright we've had in America" seems like the gross exaggeration of an elder man in Madison Avenue advertising who is trying too hard to help a younger colleague make a quick ascent to fame and fortune.[34]

Perhaps we can best sum up Albee's reputation as a controversial playwright by noting more modestly that, although he has been "condemned by some and worshipped by others, Edward Albee is clearly the most compelling American playwright to explode upon the Broadway stage since Tennessee Williams and Arthur Miller in the mid-forties."[35]

Notes and References

Chapter 1

1. Mary Lukas, "Who Isn't Afraid of Edward Albee?" *Show* (February, 1963), 83.
2. W. J. Weatherby, "Do You Like Cats?" *Manchester Guardian* (June 19, 1962), 7. Henry Hewes, ed., *The Best Plays of 1962–63* (New York, 1963), p. 74.
3. Anonymous, "Edward (Franklin) Albee," *Current Biography,* XXIV (February, 1963), 1. Page references are to the bound volume, which has a slightly different pagination from the originally issued separate magazine. Hereafter anonymous, "Albee."
4. Unpaged obituary clipping from New York *Herald Tribune* (August 3, 1961), in Theater Collection of New York Public Library (NYPL hereafter).
5. *Ibid.* and an unidentifiable newspaper clipping in same collection.
6. Anonymous, "Albee, Odd Man In On Broadway," *Newsweek,* LXI (February 4, 1963), 51. The Manhattan telephone directory for 1967 gives her business address as 630 Fifth Avenue.
7. Lukas, p. 83. See Thomas B. Morgan, "Angry Playwright in a Soft Spell," *Life,* LXII (May 26, 1967), 90 ff., for more recent information.
8. *Ibid.,* for this and the remainder of the paragraph.
9. *Ibid.* See also Arthur Gelb, "Dramatists Deny Nihilistic Trend," *New York Times,* Monday (February 15, 1960), 23.
10. Anonymous, "Albee, Odd Man In On Broadway," p. 1. Also, David Newman, "Four Make a Wave," *Esquire,* LV (April, 1961), 48.
11. Anonymous, "Albee," p. 1.
12. *Ibid.* and Newman, p. 48. Also Hewes, p. 74. See *New Yorker* (March 25, 1961), pp. 7, 31, for Albee's personal reactions to Valley Forge Military Academy and other schools.
13. Anonymous, "Albee," p. 2.
14. Anonymous, "Albee, Odd Man In On Broadway," p. 49.
15. *Ibid.,* p. 51. Lukas, p. 113, says he wrote poems, plays, stories, and a 538-page novel while at Choate.
16. Anonymous, "Albee, Odd Man In On Broadway," p. 51.

17. *Ibid.*

18. Gelb, p. 23. See John Skow, "Broadway's Hottest Playwright, Edward Albee," *Saturday Evening Post,* CCXXXVII (January 18, 1964), 33.

19. Hewes, p. 74; anonymous, "Albee," p. 2; and "Albee, Odd Man In On Broadway," p. 51.

20. Lukas, p. 113.

21. *Ibid.,* pp. 113–14. Edward Kosner, "Social Critics, Like Prophets, Are Often Honored From Afar," *New York Post* (March 31, 1961), 38.

22. Skow, p. 33. See also Weatherby, p. 7.

23. At least one anonymous critic has complained that Albee appears greatly preoccupied with the subject of *death* in his plays. See "Towards a Theatre of Cruelty?" *Times Literary Supplement,* No. 3, 235 (February 27, 1964), 166. See, too, William Flanagan, "Albee in the Village," New York *Herald Tribune* (October 27, 1963), 27, for remonstrance against somewhat misleading newspaper images of Albee as a down-and-outer.

24. *New Yorker* (March 25, 1961), p. 7. Albee was living at this time with Flanagan in a ground-floor, six-room apartment on West Twelfth Street.

25. Jerry Tallmer, "Edward Albee, Playwright," *New York Post,* Sunday Magazine section (November 4, 1962), 10.

26. Lukas, p. 113; Weatherby, p. 7.

27. Flanagan, p. 27, for all quotations in this and the preceding paragraph.

28. Hewes, p. 74; Skow, p. 33; and "Albee, Odd Man In On Broadway," p. 52.

29. Skow, p. 32. Untitled, unsigned interview in *New Yorker* (March 25, 1961), 31. Was living at this time in an apartment at 238 West Fourth Street.

30. Edward Albee, *The Zoo Story, The Death of Bessie Smith, The Sandbox* (New York, 1960), p. 4.

31. Anonymous, "Albee," p. 2. Albee's first four successful plays were produced off Broadway.

32. "Off Broadway," in *The Best Plays of 1959–60,* edited by Louis Kronenberger (New York, 1960), p. 39.

33. Lukas, p. 114.

34. Skow, p. 33.

35. Henry Hewes, ed., *The Best Plays of 1961–62* (New York, 1962), p. 323.

36. See Edward Parone, ed., *New Theatre in America* (New York, 1965), pp. 2–13. Otis L. Guernsey, *The Best Plays of 1965–66* (New York, 1966), p. 35, noted that Theater 1966—the Albee-Barr-

Wilder-New Playwrights Unit Workshop—had received a Rockefeller grant of $197,000 "for the purpose of presenting deserving off-off-Broadway *[sic]* scripts at the Cherry Lane Theater."

37. The word *wound* seems appropriate. Cf. John E. Booth, "Albee and Schneider Observe: Something's Stirring," *Theatre Arts*, XLV (March, 1961), 24, who quotes Albee as saying: "It would seem to me only logical that people . . . should come out of the theatre having *suffered* [my italics] an experience of some sort. . . . The most gratifying moment I ever had in my brief experience in the theatre was after the première of *The Zoo Story* in Berlin. When the play ended and there was forty-five seconds of absolute silence. And then people applauded. Now that silence . . . was very nice."

38. Robert Brustein, "Fragments from a Cultural Explosion," *New Republic*, CXLIV (March 27, 1961), 30.

39. "Which Is the Victim?" a letter to the editor of *The Village Voice* (September 20, 1962), 4, defending Albee from an attack by Mr. Charles Marowitz.

40. Anonymous, "Albee, Odd Man In On Broadway," p. 50.

41. Anonymous, "Albee," p. 3. Morgan, p. 99. See also unsigned review of *Ballad* in *America*, CX (January 4, 1964), 26, and Tallmer, p. 10.

42. *New York Times*, Wednesday (December 4, 1963). See issue of November 15, pp. 1 and 5 (column 4), and issue of November 1 of same year for rest of paragraph. Clipping of Louis Calta, "Albee Leaving for Soviet to Join Steinbeck in Cultural Exchange." (November 1 issue).

43. Article signed J. K., "Le dramaturge Américain Edward Albee à Varsovie." *Le Théâtre en Pologne*, monthly bulletin of the Polish Centre of the International Theatre Institute (February, 1964), 19. English translation on p. 25.

44. See *New York Times* for June 6, 1961. Unpaged clippings in the Theatre Collection, NYPL, for this and the previous date. Anonymous, "Albee," p. 2 for the quote.

45. Unpaged clippings from New York *Daily News* (May 10, 1960), in Theater Collection, NYPL. Albee was cited for "the freshness of concept and manner and the dramatic tension of The Zoo Story" which "won the immediate endorsement of reviewers and audiences sympathetic to the experimental theatre. . . ." See, also, *Esquire* News Release (April 15, 1963), p. 4, in connection with Princeton Symposium; News Release of Howard Atlee Associates (July 9, 1963); New York *Post* (May 7, 1963), p. 3; and another news clipping (September 7, 1962)—all in Theater Collection of NYPL.

46. Skow, p. 33. See *New York Post* (May 7, 1963), p. 3, for details of this disgraceful action.

47. Television interview with Albee on "Today Show" (September 26, 1966).

48. Weatherby, p. 7.

Chapter 2

1. Edward Albee, "Which Theater Is the Absurd One?" *New York Times Magazine* (February 25, 1962), 64.

2. *Ibid.*

3. *Ibid.*, p. 30. Also quoted in *Dramatist's Bulletin*, II, no. 7 (April, 1962), 1.

4. Albee, "Which Theater Is the Absurd One?" p. 64.

5. Letter of R. C. Munroe to Editor in *Newsweek* (February 18, 1963).

6. Henry Hewes, "Off Broadway," in *The Best Plays of 1960–61*, edited by Louis Kronenberger (New York, 1961), p. 47. Also, anonymous, "Albee," p. 2, and Arthur Gelb, *New York Times* (October 26, 1960), p. 44.

7. Edward Albee, *The American Dream; The Death of Bessie Smith; Fam and Yam* (New York, 1962), p. 80.

8. *Ibid.*

9. *Ibid.*, p. 81.

10. *Ibid.*, p. 82.

11. *Ibid.*, pp. 82–83.

12. *Ibid.*, p. 83.

13. *Ibid.*, p. 84.

14. *Ibid.*, p. 85.

15. *Ibid.*, pp. 85–86.

16. *Ibid.*, p. 87.

17. *Ibid.*, p. 84, for this and p. 85 for remaining quotes in paragraph.

18. Press Conference on *Tiny Alice* with Albee, held at the Billy Rose Theater [?], New York City, Monday, March 22, 1965, for all quotes in this and preceding four paragraphs. See "Transcript of Opening Remarks," issued to press.

19. Anonymous, "Visiting Scholar Series Extended," *Pratt Institute Quarterly News*, I, 1 (March, 1963), 1.

20. A[rnold] G[ingrich], in "Publisher's Page" section, an article entitled "A Lively and Responsive Weekend at Princeton," *Esquire*, LX, 1 (July, 1963), 111.

21. Press transcript of interview on *Tiny Alice* for all quotes in this paragraph and the preceding one.

22. Clipping from *New York Times* (February 18, 1963), entitled "The Critics Meet the Playwrights," by Brian O'Doherty, in NYPL Theater Collection. This account describes a symposium in which

Schneider and Albee participated at the YM-YWHA in New York.

23. Albee, "Which Theater Is the Absurd One?" p. 64.
24. *Ibid.*, p. 31.
25. Quoted in *ibid.*, but see also Martin Esslin, *The Theatre of the Absurd* (New York, 1961), p. 316.
26. Albee, "Which Theater Is the Absurd One?" p. 31.
27. *Ibid.* p. 30, for both quotations.
28. *Ibid.*, p. 66.
29. *Ibid.*, for this and the following quote.
30. See p. 7 and continuation of article on a second unpaged clipping in NYPL Theater Collection.
31. Anonymous, "Talk with the Author," *Newsweek*, LX (October 29, 1962), 53.
32. Anonymous, "Talk with the Author," p. 53.
33. Lukas, p. 114.
34. Anonymous, "Albee," pp. 1, 3.
35. Anonymous, "Towards a Theatre of Cruelty?" *Times Literary Supplement*, no. 3,235 (February 27, 1964), 166.
36. *Ibid.*
37. Edward Albee, "What's It About?—A Playwright Tries to Tell," New York *Herald Tribune Magazine* (January 22, 1961), 5.
38. Edward Albee, "Who's Afraid of the Truth?" *New York Times* (August 18, 1963), Sunday section 2 (drama), 1.
39. *Three Plays by Noel Coward*, introduction by Edward Albee (New York, 1965), p. 5, for both quotes.
40. *Ibid.*, p. 4.
41. *Ibid.*, pp. 4, 5.
42. *Ibid.*, p. 6.
43. *Ibid.*
44. *Ibid.*, p. 5.
45. Quoted by Skow, p. 33.
46. Flanagan, "Albee in the Village," p. 27.
47. Weatherby, p. 7.
48. Anonymous, "King of Off-Broadway," *Newsweek*, LVII, no. 11 (March 13, 1961), 90.
49. Anonymous, "Albee in the Village," p. 27.
50. Two years earlier, however, Flanagan's incidental music to *The Sandbox* had succeeded.
51. Whitney Balliett, "Three Cheers for Albee," *New Yorker*, XXXVI (February 4, 1961), 66, for both quotes.
52. "Theatre," *Nation*, CXCII, no. 6 (February 11, 1961), 126. Other comments ranged from "not very successful" to "coolly received." See respectively Henry Hewes, "On Our Bad Behaviour," *Saturday Review*, XLIV (February 11, 1961), 54, and anonymous, "Albee," p. 2.

53. Anonymous, "Visiting Scholar Series Extended," *Pratt Institute Quarterly News,* I, 1 (March, 1963), 1.
54. Newman, "Four Make a Wave," *Esquire,* LV (April, 1961), 49.
55. Anonymous, "Albee," p. 3.
56. Lukas, p. 114.
57. *Ibid.*

Chapter 3

1. Edward Albee, *The Zoo Story, The Death of Bessie Smith, The Sandbox:* Three Plays, Introduced by the Author (New York, 1960), p. 11. Numbers in parentheses throughout this and the next two chapters refer to this volume.
2. The fact that Jerry here corrects himself with Peter's language seems to show his recognition of the fact that communication has been achieved.
3. Jerry had actually made contact, *briefly,* with the dog earlier. See p. 41, where he says "during that twenty seconds . . . we made contact." But this rapprochement had lapsed into indifference, in which they neither loved nor hurt each other, nor—what seems worse—any longer tried "to reach each other." P. 44.
4. I say *with irony* advisedly, because in the Bible the phrase "And it came to pass" usually refers to actions outside human control, whereas here Jerry controls, or rather instigates, the situation, however underhandedly he goes about it.
5. See Luke 22:54–62. It would be silly, of course, to identify Jerry with Jesus Christ; for, although both come unto Peter, Jerry seems to sense the vast difference between himself and Christ. And this may be the reason he laughs at his own words. For the view that Jerry represents Christ and Peter, St. Peter, see Rose A. Zimbardo, "Symbolism and Naturalism in Edward Albee's 'The Zoo Story' " *Twentieth Century Literature,* VIII (April, 1962), 14. For an even more fantastic interpretation, equating Jerry with the Ancient Mariner in Coleridge's poem (Peter becomes the wedding guest and the dog, the albatross), see Peter Spielberg, "The Albatross in Albee's Zoo," *College English,* XXVII, 7 (April, 1966), 562–65.
6. See Sartre's "Forgers of the Myth," translated by Rosamond Gilder in *Theater Arts Anthology.* Reproduced in R. W. Corrigan's *The Modern Theater* (New York, 1964), p. 782
7. Although the language may seem a little strange here, Albee prepares us with one earlier "So be it" in the mouth of Jerry (24).
8. Marjorie Grene, *Dreadful Freedom, A Critique of Existentialism* (Chicago, 1948), p. 24.
9. See Gabriel Marcel, *The Philosophy of Existentialism,* 5th paperbound edition (New York, 1965), pp. 9–46.

10. See Aristotle's *Poetics*, XIII, 2, for definitions of *pity* and *fear*.

11. See Gerald F. Else, *Aristotle's Poetics: The Argument* (Cambridge, Massachusetts, 1963), pp. 342–55, for an extended discussion of *recognition*, either with or without *reversal.*

12. Butcher translation, *Poetics,* XI, 2.

Chapter 4

1. See Joseph Wood Krutch, *The Modern Temper* (New York, 1933), chapter 5, "The Tragic Fallacy," pp. 115–44.

2. Still using Aristotelian terms, I call the plot *complex,* not because it reverses itself but because it does not. The general line of the plot is unchanged from beginning to end—Grandma dies. But the plot is complex because it contains *recognition,* or discovery—a "change from ignorance to knowledge, producing love or hate between the persons destined . . . for good or bad fortune." *Poetics,* XI, 2 (Butcher translation). Grandma discovers that the handsome young man is the Angel of Death, and she is momentarily confused because, as such, he becomes her enemy (see p. 157 of text). But this enmity (which was often the most important part of the emotional impact in older Greek tragedies—cf. Clytemnestra's recognition of Orestes in *The Libation Bearers,* for example—and which was rarely *momentary*) yields to resignation on her further discovery that the young man means to do her no harm, when in fact, he gently kisses her, and she discovers dying is a surprisingly pleasant experience.

3. Paul Cubeta, *Modern Drama for Analysis* (New York, 1962), 3rd edition, p. 603, suggests that Mommy and Daddy in their sitting, waiting, mourning, and rejoicing activities resemble the chorus in Eliot's *Murder in the Cathedral.*

4. See William Flanagan for detailed discussion of this point. "Notes on the Performance of the Musical Score for *The Sandbox,*" in Mayorga, editor, *The Best Short Plays of 1959–60,* pp. 69–70.

Chapter 5

1. Irving Howe in a lecture "What Can a Literary Critic Do?" at Tuskegee Institute, February 25, 1966.

2. Anonymous, "Towards a Theatre of Cruelty?" *Times Literary Supplement,* no. 3,235 (February 27, 1964), 166, notes that the hospital room in *Bessie Smith* is "the ironic opposite of mutual aid and altruistic love."

3. Harold Clurman, "Theatre," *Nation,* CXCII (March 18, 1961), 242, does say, however, Albee's method in *Bessie Smith* is to "help us understand its human sources" "instead of emphasizing the shameful shock of the episode [her death]."

Chapter 6

1. Edward Albee, *The American Dream* (New York, 1960 and 1961), p. 9. All parenthetical page references in this chapter refer to this text.

2. P. 8. In Dante's and Boccaccio's sense of *comedy* as a literary work that begins in a state of confusion and ends in a state of order, the play would be correctly designated a comedy.

3. *Ibid.* In this Preface Albee says he intended "a condemnation of complacency, cruelty, emasculation and vacuity. . . ."

4. Albee's technique in describing this dismemberment of the child may be interpreted as somewhat supernaturalistic or expressionistic. (Cf. Büchner's *Woyzeck,* O'Casey's *Cock-a-Doodle-Dandy,* etc.)

5. He had also lost his parents: "My mother died the night I was born and I never knew my father. . . ." (77)

Chapter 7

1. All parenthetical references are to pages in the most generally available inexpensive edition of the play, a Giant Cardinal issue of Pocket Books, Inc.—Edward Albee, *Who's Afraid of Virginia Woolf?* (New York, 1963). See pp. 3, 7.

2. George talks mainly about experimenting in genetics and the elimination of history, so that the discussion is entirely personal. In a television appearance, on the "Today Show," September 26, 1966, Albee registered his disapproval of the omission of this discussion from the movie of the play, which starred Elizabeth Taylor and Richard Burton.

3. The games continue, of course, in the last two acts. See below in text.

4. See Elder Olson, *Tragedy and the Theory of the Drama* (Detroit, 1961), 241–42, for extended definition of *seriousness.*

5. Mitford M. Mathews, *A Dictionary of Americanisms on Historical Principles* (Chicago, 1951), p. 92, gives for beanbag "a small bag filled with beans used in children's games."

6. *Poetics,* XVIII, I (Butcher translation).

7. In his use of the concept, or device, of *exorcism,* Albee seems to have drawn a page from Antonin Artaud's *The Theater and Its Double,* translated by Mary Caroline Richards (New York, 1958), 60. See pp. 31–32 for a more extensive statement of the effect of the theater on its audience.

8. See Else's excellent discussion of *recognition* (or discovery), pp. 348–55.

Chapter 8

1. Robert Brustein, "The Playwright as Impersonater," *New Republic,* CXLIX (November 16, 1963), 28; anonymous, "Lonesome Lovers," *Time,* LXXXII (November 8, 1963), 67; Watts, *New York Theatre Critics' Reviews,* XXIV (1963), 212; Hewes, *The Best Plays of 1963–64,* p. 6. All parenthetical pages refer to Edward Albee, *The Ballad of the Sad Cafe* (New York, 1963).

2. Sam Zolotow, " 'Malcolm' to Quit Saturday Night," *New York Times* (January 13, 1966), 46L. Richard Barr estimated the loss at $100,000. All parenthetical references in text are to Edward Albee, *Malcolm* (New York, 1966).

3. Albee, "Who Is James Purdy?" *New York Times,* Sunday drama section 2 (January 9, 1966), © 1967 by the *New York Times* Company. Reprinted by permission.

4. Walter Kerr, *New York Theatre Critics' Review,* XXVII, no. 1 (January 16, 1966), p. 394.

5. Clive Barnes, "The Theater: 'Everything in the Garden' Arrives" *New York Times* (November 30, 1967), p. 60. Cf. Albee, "The Future Belongs to Youth," *New York Times,* Sunday drama section 2 (November 26, 1967), pp. 1, 7. Albee's adaptation of Truman Capote's *Breakfast at Tiffany's* never reached production in 1966. See Barbara La Fontaine, "Triple Threat On, Off and Off-Off Broadway," *New York Times* (February 25, 1968), 36ff., for further discussion of Albee's adaptations.

Chapter 9

1. Information on *wayang* is very hard to come by, and my only source is a folder on this subject picked up at the New York World's Fair (1964–65) and printed by P. N. F. B. of Djakarta, Indonesia. A member of the Indonesian Embassy in Washington, D. C., knew of no work in English on this subject, but did volunteer that there was a book on it in Russian. It is well known, of course, that Artaud's *The Theater and Its Double,* pp. 53–73, drew many of its ideas from the Indonesian theater.

2. See Press conference transcript of Albee's opening remarks (New York City, Monday, March 22, 1965, at the Billy Rose Theater), p. 5. Reprinted in the *Dramatists' Guild Quarterly,* according to Guernsey, *Best Plays of 1964–65,* p. 251n.

3. *Ibid.,* pp. 5–6.

4. Cf. Sören Kierkegaard's concept of Christianity as "the personal experience of an isolated individual." See Lillian Hornstein *et al., The Reader's Companion to World Literature* (New York, 1956), p. 244.

5. Albee's Press Conference, p. 5.

6. *Ibid.*, pp. 6, 7.

7. Parenthetical references in this chapter are to Edward Albee, *Tiny Alice* (New York, 1965).

8. Albee's Press Conference, p. 5.

9. See Ruth Eva Schulz-Seitz, *Edward Albee, der Dichterphilosoph der Bühne* (Frankfurt, 1966), pp. 11–16, 33–39, 41–64, for a discussion of thematic similarities and differences between the two plays.

10. See *The Balcony, Deathwatch, The Maids, The Blacks,* and *The Screens.*

11. Cf. Genet's *The Maids.*

12. Schulz-Seitz, p. 21, "Der Rechtsanwalt ist, oder möchte sein, der personifizierte Verstand." (The lawyer is, or might be, Reason personified.) See also p. 32. For this author's comment on Julian as a representative of Faith, but faith entirely separated from illusion or anthropomorphism, see pp. 23–24.

13. I use the word *sublimity* here with special reference to its meaning in Longinus and in Edmund Burke.

Chapter 10

1. Edward Albee, *A Delicate Balance* (New York, 1966), unnumbered page preceding text and p. 3. Parenthetical page references are to this text.

Chapter 11

1. Respectively "Theatre," *Nation,* CXC (February 13, 1960), 153; "Benchmanship," *Saturday Review,* XLIII (February 6, 1960), 32; and *The Theatre of Protest and Paradox* (New York, 1964), 277.

2. See, for example, Tom F. Driver, "What's the Matter with Edward Albee?" *Reporter,* XXX (January 2, 1964), 38; Esslin, p. 226; and Clurman, p. 153. Wellwarth, pp. 277–78; Robert Brustein, "Krapp and a Little Claptrap," *New Republic,* CXLII (February 22, 1960), 22.

3. Brustein, "Krapp and Claptrap," p. 22; Esslin, pp. 31, 226; anonymous, "Towards a Theatre of Cruelty?" p. 166; and Allan Lewis, "The Fun and Games of Edward Albee," *Theatre Journal,* XI (March, 1964), 30, 31.

4. Cubeta, pp. 599, 600, 602–3.

5. *Ibid.*, p. 599.

6. Cf. Allan Lewis, pp. 27, 33; Cubeta, p. 602; Anthony West, "The Subhuman Theatre," *Show* (July, 1962), 27; Skow, p. 19; and Elizabeth C. Phillips, "Albee and the Theatre of the Absurd," *Tennessee Studies in Literature,* X (1965), 76.

7. Respectively Wellwarth, p. 278; Thomas Prideaux, "The Albee Attitude," *Life,* LIII (December 14, 1962), 110; Lukas, p. 114.

8. Roger Gellert, "Albee et al.," *New Statesman*, LXII, 1959 (November 3, 1961), 667–68; Whitney Balliett, "Empress of the Blues," *New Yorker*, XXXVII (March 11, 1961), 114; Gellert, p. 668.

9. Prideaux, "The Albee Attitude," p. 110. James Baldwin's "Theatre; The Negro In and Out," in John A. Williams, ed., *The Angry Black* (New York, 1962), 21.

10. Allan Lewis, p. 31; anonymous, "Towards a Theatre of Cruelty?" p. 166, *et al.;* Balliett, "Empress," p. 114, regarded the Nurse as a symbol of the modern South, a highly doubtful interpretation.

11. See, among others, anonymous, "Farce from Ionesco," *Time*, LXXVII (February 3, 1961), 55; Hewes, "On Our Bad Behavior," *Saturday Review*, XLVI (February 11, 1961), 54; Phillips, p. 78; anonymous, "Albee," p. 3; and Otto Reinert, *Drama, An Introductory Anthology* (Boston, 1964), alternate edition, 869–70.

12. Robert Hatch, "Arise Ye Playgoers of the World," *Horizon*, III, 6 (July, 1961), 117; Tom Driver, "A Milestone and a Fumble," *Christian Century*, LVIII (March 1, 1961), 275; Reinert, p. 868.

13. Driver, "A Milestone and a Fumble," p. 275; Whitney Balliett, "Three Cheers for Albee," *New Yorker*, XXXVI (February 4, 1961), 64; Clurman, "Theatre," *Nation* (February 11, 1961), pp. 125, 126.

14. Tom Driver, "What's the Matter with Edward Albee?" *Reporter*, XXX (January 2, 1964), 39.

15. Emil Roy, "Who's Afraid of Virginia Woolf and the Tradition?" *Bucknell Review*, XIII (March, 1965), 27–36.

16. Diana Trilling, "Who's Afraid of the Culture Elite?" *Esquire*, LX (December, 1963), 74, 69, 76.

17. *Ibid.*

18. See Coleman, Nadel, Chapman, Taubman, and various critics in *New York Theatre Critics' Reviews* (1962), pp. 251–54; John McCarten, "Long Night's Journey Into Daze," *New Yorker*, XXXVIII (October 20, 1962), 85, *et al.*

19. Chapman, Kerr *et al.* in *New York Theatre Critics' Reviews* (1962), pp. 251–52; Leonard Pronko, *Avant Garde* (Berkeley, 1961), pp. 7, 80, 84; *et al.*

20. See *New York Theatre Critics' Reviews*, XXVII, no. 1 (January 16, 1966), 392–94; Robert Brustein, "Albee's Allegory of Innocence," *New Republic*, CLIV (January 29, 1966), 36. For a representative sample of *Ballad* reviews, see: Clurman, "Theatre," *Nation* (November 23, 1963), p. 353; John McCarten, "Tormented Trio," *New Yorker*, XXXIX (November 9, 1963), 95; *New York Theatre Critics' Reviews*, XXIV, no. 16 (1963), 212–15.

21. See, among others, Harold Clurman, "Tiny Alice; Hughie," *Nation*, CC (January 18, 1965), 65; Howard Taubman, "Theatre: Albee's 'Tiny Alice' Opens," *New York Times* (December 30, 1964),

14; Henry Hewes, "The Tiny Alice Caper," *Saturday Review*, XLVIII (January 30, 1965), 38; R. S. Stewart, "John Gielgud and Edward Albee Talk About the Theater," *Atlantic*, CCX (April, 1965), 68; anonymous, "Chinese Boxes," *Newsweek*, LXV (January 11, 1965), 75; and Wilfred Sheed, "The Stage," *Commonweal*, LXXXI (January 22, 1965), 543–44.

22. Clurman, "Theatre," *Nation* (October 10, 1966), pp. 361–63, and Brustein, "Albee Decorates an Old House," *New Republic*, CLV (October 8, 1966), 35–36.

23. Brustein, "Albee Decorates an Old House," p. 35; Hewes, "The Family That Stayed Separate," *Saturday Review*, XLIX (October 8, 1966), 90; Walter Kerr, "The Theater: Albee's 'A Delicate Balance,'" *New York Times* (September 23, 1966), 44L; and Gerald Weales, "Stop the Balance, I Want to Get Off," *Reporter*, XXXV (October 20, 1966), 53.

24. Kerr, "The Theater: Albee's 'A Delicate Balance,'" p. 44L; Brustein, "Albee Decorates an Old House," p. 36; Weales, "Stop the Balance," p. 52; and anonymous, "Skin Deep," *Newsweek*, LXVIII (October 3, 1966), 98.

25. Prideaux, p. 110. Alan Schneider, "Why So Afraid?" *Tulane Drama Review*, VII (Spring, 1963), 11, defends Albee against the charge of sentimentalism, arguing that he is dedicated to "smashing [the] rosy view" of the sentimentalists.

26. Richard Watts, Jr., "The High Talent of Edward Albee," *New York Post* (February 5, 1961), unpaged, clipped in NYPL Theater Collection. Skow, "Broadway's Hottest Playwright," p. 33, notes Albee's ability to produce powerful emotional effects on both actors and audience.

27. Trotta, "On Stage: Edward Albee," *Horizon*, IV, no. 1 (September, 1961), p. 79. Anonymous, "Albee," p. 3, considers Albee's belief that the playwright must be a social critic.

28. Skow, "Broadway's Hottest Playwright," p. 33.

29. Marya Mannes, "The Half-World of American Drama," *Reporter*, XXVIII (April 25, 1963), p. 50.

30. Trotta, p. 79.

31. Edward Albee, *A Delicate Balance*, p. 172.

32. *Ibid.*, and *The Best Plays of 1962–63*, p. 74.

33. John Mason Brown, *Dramatis Personae* (New York, 1963), p. 539.

34. Anonymous, "Albee, Odd Man In On Broadway," p. 50.

35. *Ibid.*, p. 49.

Selected Bibliography

(This highly selective bibliography includes neither reviews nor general material related to the "theater of the absurd" or Existentialism. These items are included, instead, in Notes and References.)

PRIMARY SOURCES

(Arranged chronologically)

1. *Plays*

The Zoo Story and *The Sandbox; Two Short Plays.* New York: Dramatists' Play Service, 1960.

"The Zoo Story." *Evergreen Review,* No. 12 (March–April, 1960). Pp. 28–52.

The Zoo Story, The Death of Bessie Smith, The Sandbox, Three Plays, Introduced by the Author. New York: Coward-McCann, 1960.

The American Dream. New York: Coward-McCann, 1961.

The American Dream; The Death of Bessie Smith; Fam and Yam. New York: Dramatists' Play Service, 1962.

Who's Afraid of Virginia Woolf? New York: Atheneum, 1962.

Who's Afraid of Virginia Woolf? New York: Pocket Books, 1963–64.

The Play "The Ballad of the Sad Cafe": *Carson McCullers' Novella Adapted to the Stage.* Boston: Houghton Mifflin, 1963, and New York: Atheneum, 1963.

Tiny Alice. New York: Atheneum, 1965.

Malcolm. New York: Atheneum, 1966.

A Delicate Balance. New York: Atheneum, 1966.

Everything in the Garden. New York: Atheneum, 1968.

2. *Articles*

"What's It About?—A Playwright Tries to Tell." New York *Herald Tribune Magazine,* "The Lively Arts" (January 22, 1961), 5. Interviewed by a lady reporter from Buenos Aires, Albee talks about *The American Dream* and *Bartleby* and expresses his gratitude to the public.

"Which Theatre Is the Absurd One?" *New York Times Magazine* (February 25, 1962), 30–31, 64, 66. Defense of the Theater of the Absurd. Attacks the existing Broadway theater, which he calls the "absurd" one.

"Just What Is the Theater of the Absurd?" *Dramatists' Bulletin,* II, no. 7 (April 1962), 1–2. Quotes from preceding *New York Times Magazine* article.

"Novel Beginning." *Esquire,* LX (July 1963), 59–60. Excerpt from a novel in which Albee tries to fuse stream-of-consciousness technique, à la Virginia Woolf, with stage dialogue.

"Who's Afraid of the Truth?" *New York Times,* Sunday drama section (August 18, 1963), 1.

Three Plays by Noel Coward, Introduction by Edward Albee. New York: Dell Publishing Co., 1965.

"Who Is James Purdy?" *New York Times,* Sunday drama section (January 9, 1966), 1, 3. Discusses problems of adapting for the stage. Written on the eve of Albee's production of *Malcolm.* Pleads for wider reading of Purdy's works.

"Creativity and Commitment." *Saturday Review,* XLIX (June 4, 1966), 26. Short article occasioned by international P.E.N. conference in New York.

SECONDARY SOURCES

(Arranged alphabetically)

1. *Books*

Blum, Daniel, editor. *Theatre World, 1961–62,* Vol. 18. New York: Chilton Co., 1962. Contains pictures, programs, and runs of season's plays.

Brustein, Robert. *The Theatre of Revolt: An Approach to Modern Drama.* Boston: Little, Brown and Co., 1964. Relates Albee to Existential revolt and to Pirandello theme of conflict between illusion and reality. Final chapter deals with Artaud, Genet, and "The Theatre of Cruelty."

Esslin, Martin. *The Theatre of the Absurd.* Garden City, New York: Doubleday, 1961. Best treatment to date. Brief discussion of *The Zoo Story, The Death of Bessie Smith,* and *The American Dream* and of their relationship to work of Pinter and Ionesco. Short bibliography of Albee.

Cubeta, Paul M. *Modern Drama for Analysis.* 3rd edition. New York: Holt, Rinehart & Winston, 1962. Discerning analysis of *The Sandbox.*

Debusscher, Gilbert. *Edward Albee: Tradition and Renewal.* Translated from the French by Anne W. Williams. Brussels, Belgium: American Studies Center, 1967. Published as my manuscript was being readied for printer. At first reading, I find it a thoughtful study.

FINKELSTEIN, SIDNEY. *Existentialism and Alienation in American Literature.* New York: International Publishers, 1965. Excellent short analyses of *Virginia Woolf* and *Tiny Alice.*

FLANAGAN, WILLIAM. "Notes on the Performance of the Musical Score for *The Sandbox.*" *The Best Short Plays of 1959–60.* Edited by Margaret Mayorga. Boston: Beacon Press, 1960.

GASSNER, JOHN. *Directions in Modern Theatre and Drama.* New York: Holt, Rinehart & Winston, 1965. Contains a brief introduction to the "theater of the absurd" and reprints Albee's article "Which Theatre Is the Absurd One?"

KERR, WALTER. *The Theater in Spite of Itself.* New York: Simon and Schuster, 1963. Treats generally "The Ambiguity of the Theater of the Absurd"; discusses *Virginia Woolf.*

REINERT, OTTO. *Drama, An Introductory Anthology.* Alternate edition. Boston: Little, Brown and Co., 1964. Criticizes *The American Dream;* shows Albee's ties to the absurdist movement in the introduction.

SCHULZ-SEITZ, RUTH EVA. *Edward Albee, der Dichterphilosoph der Bühne.* Frankfurt am Main: Vittorio Klostermann, 1966. Treats the illusion-reality problem rather fully and well in *Tiny Alice* and *Virginia Woolf,* the two plays it discusses.

2. *Dissertation*

RULE, MARGARET, "Edward Albee in Germany." Unpublished Ph.D. dissertation in progress at English Department of University of Arkansas. Treats productions of Albee's plays in Germany and his reputation there.

3. *Articles*

(See under Notes and References.)

4. *Bibliography*

RULE, MARGARET. "An Edward Albee Bibliography," *Twentieth Century Literature,* XIV (April, 1968), 35–45. Contains about 300 items. Mrs. Rule and I have compiled an extension of this bibliography—about 1,000 entries, including articles and reviews in foreign languages—which we plan to publish as a monograph.

Index

Aeschylus, 74
Ahab, 152
Albee, Edward, Preface; chron.; contents; early life, 15; early contact with actors, 16; formal ed., 16-17; early role as actor, 17; early odd jobs, 17-18; maternal grandmother, 17; encouragement from Thornton Wilder, 19; writing and early success of *Zoo Story*, 19; 1962 campaign for theater of absurd, 19-20; support of other playwrights, 20; hobbies, 21; playwright workshop, 21; lectures (home and abroad), 21-22; four plays Off-Broadway in 1963-64, 21-22; visit to Italy (1964), 22; popularity in Germany, 23; prizes, 23; on the American character, 24; current popularity, 24; literary and art theory (including *Fam and Yam*), 25-39; on TV, 28; on audience and critic, 28-31; early social realism, 32; favorite playwrights, 36; music, 37-38; cost of plays, 38-39; adaptations, chap. 8 (109-29); appraisal of work by critics, chap. 11 (165-170)

WRITINGS OF:
Aliqueen, chron., 16
American Dream, The, chron., 22, 23, 32, 35, 37, 39, 75-81, 165, 166, 167, 168
Ballad of the Sad Cafe, The, chron., 20, 22, 109-119, 128, 166
Bartleby, the Scrivener, chron., 38, 167
Box-Mao-Box, chron.
Death of Bessie Smith, The, chron., 22, 23, 32, 39, 62-74, 166
Delicate Balance, A, chron., 154-64, 167, 168
Everything in the Garden, chron., 167
Fam and Yam, chron., 26-28
Jumbo, 16
Malcolm, chron., 109, 119-129, 167
"Nihilist," 16
Sandbox, The, 19, 20, 32, 38, 39, 55-61, 75, 165
Schism, 17
Tiny Alice, chron., 20, 26, 30, 31, 130-153, 167, 168
Who's Afraid of Virginia Woolf? chron., 20, 22, 24, 35, 37, 38, 39, 62, 82-108, 109, 136, 139, 166, 167, 168
Zoo Story, The, 17, 18, 19, 20, 22, 23, 27, 28, 32, 38, 39, 40-54, 165, 167

WORK IN PROSPECT:
All Over, 169
Life and Death, 169
Seascape, 169
Substitute Speaker, The, 169

Albee, Edward Franklin (adopted grandfather), 15
Albee, Frances, 15
Albee, Reed A., 15
Alger, Horatio, 15
American National Theater and Academy, 24
American Theatre Wing, 24
Anderson, Maxwell, 17
ANTA (N.Y.) Matinee Theatre Series, 26
Antoinette Perry Awards, 24
Aristophanes, 35
Aristotle, Preface, 50, 54, 60, 61, 101
Arizona, 16
Arrabal, Fernando, 20, 32, 36
Artaud, Antonin, 130, 153

Bald Soprano, The (Ionesco), 166
Baldwin, James, 166
Balinese theater, 130
Balliett, Whitney, 166
Barghoorn, F. C., 22

Barlog, Boleslaw, 19
Barr, Richard, 19, 20, 39
Baudelaire, Pierre Charles, 41
Beatrice and Benedick (Shakespeare's *Much Ado*), 82
Beckett, Samuel, 19, 20, 23, 32, 36, 41, 149, 165
Beethoven, Ludwig van, 30
Berlin, 19, 25, 167
Bertha (Koch), 20
Best Foreign Play Awards (Buenos Aires), 23
Betti, Ugo, 36
Bible, 49-50
Billy Rose Theater, 30, 39
Blithe Spirit (Coward), 36
Bloomingdale's, 18
Braque, Georges, 27, 28
Braun, Pinkas, 19
Brave New World (A. Huxley), 89
Brecht, Bertolt, 26, 36
Broadway-Hollywood theater, 20, 25-39 (passim)
Brocken, 92
Brown, John Mason, 24
Brustein, Robert, 21, 165, 167
Buenos Aires (experimental theater), 25
Buenos Aires, University of, 21

Camus, Albert, 32, 37, 52
Caretaker, The (Pinter), 167
Carousel (Rodgers and Hammerstein), 30
Carthage, 86
Chekhov, Anton, 26, 33, 166
Chelsea, 18
Cherry Lane Theater, 19, 23, 32
Choate Literary Magazine, 17
Choate School, The, chron.
Christ, 49
Ciardi, John, 21
Circle in the Square Theater School, 21
Clark, Bobby, 37
Clurman, Harold, 38, 165, 166, 167
Cocktail Party, The (Eliot), 167
Columbia University, 27
Columbia University Board of Trustees, 24
Cooper, Giles, chron., 167
Coward, Noel, 36
Cubeta, Paul, 165
Czechoslovakia, 22

Dali, Salvador, 38
Deathwatch (Genet), 20
De Chirico, Giorgio, 38
Decline of the West, The (Spengler), 99
Diamond, David, 19
Dido and Aeneas, 86
Dionysian Revels, 101
Doctor of Literature (hon.), chron.
Dog that Bit People, The (Thurber), 43
Drama Critics Award, chron.
Dryden, Preface
Durante, Jimmy, 16

Eliot, T. S., 167, 169
Embers (Beckett), 26
Emerson College (Boston), chron.
Endgame (Beckett), 20
Essay of Dramatic Poesy, An (Dryden), Preface
Esslin, Martin, 31-32, 37
Euripides, 74, 166
Evergreen Review, 26, bibliog.
Existentialism, 32, 34, 37, 51, 52, 130, 144, 153

Family Reunion, The (Eliot), 167
Fascism, 35, 65, 70
Fields, W. C., 37
Flanagan, William, 18, 19, 20, 37, 38
Florence, 22
Florida, 16
Foreign Press Association Award, 23
Forever Amber (Windsor), 30
France, Anatole, 86
Frankenstein(ian) horror, 37
French avant-garde, 32
French Impressionism, 33
Freud, Sigmund, 41

Gallows Humor (Richardson), 20
Gassner, John, 24

Gelber, Jack, 27
Genet, Jean, 20, 23, 32, 36, 41, 139, 166
Gielgud, Sir John, 151
Gomorrah, 86
Gorky, Maxim, 153
Grand Canyon Suite (Grofé), 30
Greek Tragedy, 50, 54, chap. 2 (passim), 74, 101
Greenwich Village, 17, 18, 24, 41
Grizzard, George, 39
Grofé, Ferde, 30

Hagen, Uta, 39
Harkness Theater (Columbia Univ.), 21
Hartz Mts., 92
Hay Fever (Coward), 36
Hayes, Joseph, 35
Hellman, Lillian, 166
Hewes, Henry, 19, 165, 169
Hill, Arthur, 39
Hinton, James, Jr., 38
Hofstra College, 21
Hungary, 22
Hunzinger, Mrs. Stephani, 19
Huxley, Aldous, 89

Ibsen, Henrik, 26, 33, 35, 36, 166
Iceman Cometh, The (O'Neill), 153
Inge, William, 26, 27, 28
International Who's Who, 21
Ionesco, Eugene, 20, 23, 32, 36, 41, 166
Ives, Charles, 38

Jarry, Alfred, 169
Jones, LeRoi, 20
Jung, Carl, 166

Kafka, Franz, 166
Kalcheim, Lee, 20
Kaleidoscope (Texas), 16
Kant, Immanuel, 51
Keith-Albee Theater Circuit, 15
Kerr, Walter, 30, 128, 165
Killer, The (Ionesco), 20
Klein, [Yves?], 27, 28 (possibly Franz Kline)
Koch, Kenneth, 20, 32
Kopit, Arthur, 21, 27
Krapp's Last Tape (Beckett), 19, 165
Krutch, Joseph W., 60

Lahr, Bert, 37
Larchmont, N. Y., chron.
Lawrenceville School, The, chron., 16
Lerner, Max, 21
Little, Stuart, 39
Lola d'Annunzio prize, 23
London, 25
London, Jack, 166
Long Island Sound, 16
Lot, 86
Lover, The (Pinter), 20
Lower Depths, The (Gorky), 153
Lukas, Mary, 21

MacDowell Colony (Peterborough, N. H.), 19
Male Animal, The (Thurber), 37
Manhattan Towers Hotel, 18
Marcel, Gabriel, 52
Marquand, J. P., 41
Marx, Groucho, 37
Masque of Kings, The (Anderson), 17
Mastroianni, Marcello, 22
McCullers, Carson, chron., 109, 166
Melville, Herman, 38
Miami Beach, 16
Miller, Arthur, 23, 27, 28, 170
Moby Dick, 152
Modigliani, Amedeo, 27, 28
Molière, 35
Montauk, L. I., 24
Motherwell, [R. B.?], 27, 28
Much Ado About Nothing (Shakespeare), 82

Nekros (H. Tierney), 26
New Testament, 49
New York Drama Critics, 24
New York Repertory, 21
New York Writers Conference (Wagner College), 21
No Exit (Sartre), 73

Index

Obie Award, 23
O'Casey, Sean, 26
Oedipus (complex), 96
Off-Broadway, 19, 26, 32
O'Neill, Eugene, 19, 23, 153, 166, 167, 168
Orestes (complex), 96
Osgood, Lawrence, 20
Our Town (Wilder), 56
Outer Circle Award, 24

Palm Beach, 16
Penguin Island (France), 86
Perr, Harvey, 20
Peter (apostle), 49
Picnic on the Battlefield (Arrabal), 20
Pidgeon, Walter, 16
Pinter, Harold, 20, 36
Pirandello, Luigi, 26, 56
Platonism, 141, 148
Play (Beckett), 20
Poe, E. A., 160
Poetics (Aristotle), 45
Poland, 22
Pound, Ezra, 169
Pratt Institute, 38
Prideaux, Tom, 166
Princeton Response Weekend (*Esquire Mag.*), 21, 30-31
Private Lives (Coward), 36
Producer Theater, 19
Provincetown Playhouse, 19
Pryce-Jones, Alan, 21
Pulitzer prize for drama, chron., 164
Purdy, James, chron., 109, 119, 128

Remembrance of Things Past (Proust), 30
Respectful Prostitute, The (Sartre), 74
Richardson, Jack, 20, 27, 32
Rockwell, Norman, 30
Rome, 22
Room, The (Pinter), 167
Ross, Lillian, 33
Roy, Emil, 166
Rye Country Day School, chron.

Sackler, Howard, 20
Sardou, Viktorien, 154
Sartre, Jean Paul, 32, 51, 52
Schiller Theater *Werkstatt,* 19
Schneider, Alan, 19, 20, 31, 39
Scribe, Augustin E., 154
Shakespeare, William, 26
Shaw, G. B., 26, 35
Simon, John, 21
Six Characters in Search of an Author (Pirandello), 56
Social Realism, 32
Sophocles, 74
Soutine, Cham, 30
Soviet Union (Russia)—Leningrad, Odessa, Kiev, Moscow, 22
Spengler, Oswald, 99
State Department, U. S., 22
Stein, Gertrude, 166
Steinbeck, John, 22
Streetcar Named Desire, A (Williams), 103
Strindberg, August, 26, 166
Surrealism, chap. 9 (130-153), 165, 169

Taming of the Shrew, The (Shakespeare), 82
Theater of the Absurd, 19, 20, 31, 32, 33, 167
Theater of the Absurd Reportory Company, 32
Theatre de Lys (N. Y.), 26
Theatre 1960, 19
Theatre 1964, 20
Thurber, James, 37, 43
Tierney, Harry, 26
Tonight We Improvise (Pirandello), 56
Trilling, Diana, 166
Trinity College, chron.
Twelfth Night (Shakespeare), 86

Ubu Roi (Jarry), 169

Valley Forge Military Academy, chron.
Vaudeville (hellsapoppin), 37

Vernon Rice Award, 23
Vertical and Horizontal (Ross), 33

Waiting for Godot (Beckett), 149
Walpurgisnacht, 92, 100, 101
Warsaw University, 22
Warwick and Legler, 17
Washington, D. C., chron.
Washington and Lee University, 21
Watts, Richard, 165
Wayang (Indonesian), 130, 153
Wellwarth, George, 165
Westchester Co., 16
Western Union, 18
White Plains, N. Y., 15
Whitehead, Robert, 21
Wilder, Clinton, 19, 20, 39
Wilder, Thornton, 19, 23, 27, 28, 56
Williams, Tennessee, 18, 23, 27, 28, 103, 166, 170
Würzburg University, 23
Wynn, Ed, 16

Yevtushenko, Yevgenii, 22, 30

Zeffirelli, Franco, 22